STANDARD GAUGE GREAT WESTERN 4-4-0s
PART 1
INSIDE-CYLINDER CLASSES 1894—1910

The most famous of all Great Western 4-4-0s: No 3440
City of Truro at Westbourne Park sheds.

STANDARD GAUGE
GREAT WESTERN 4-4-0s
PART 1
INSIDE-CYLINDER CLASSES
1894–1910

O. S. NOCK
BSc, CEng, FICE, FIMechE

DAVID & CHARLES
NEWTON ABBOT LONDON
NORTH POMFRET (VT) VANCOUVER

ISBN 0 7153 7411 7

Library of Congress Catalog Card Number 77-89376

Set in 10 on 11 English
and printed in Great Britain
by Biddles of Guildford
for David & Charles (Publishers) Limited
Brunel House Newton Abbot Devon

Published in the United States of America
by David & Charles Inc
North Pomfret Vermont 05053 USA

Published in Canada
by Douglas David & Charles Limited
1875 Welch Street North Vancouver BC

CONTENTS

One of Churchward's favourites: *Polyanthus,* built 1908.
(W. J. Reynolds)

PREFACE

This book, or rather the pair of books that will form this monograph, has been on the agenda for a long time. When Mr David St John Thomas first asked me to do it, I must admit that I stalled a little. It would be the most complicated of all the titles so far included in this series. For one thing there were no fewer than eight distinct locomotive classes to be covered, and although there were common threads of development running through them all, there were many side issues and more than one blind alley, all of which would require chronicling. The history of this group of locomotives has been ably documented in the past in the scholarly writings of F. W. Brewer in *The Railway Magazine* and by the late Hugh le Fleming in the publications of The Railway Correspondence & Travel Society. But all historians, whether writing of locomotives, or anything else, have their own particular fancies, quite apart from the 'bees in the bonnet' evident in some lighter-weight journalistic effusions. For my own part, after a life in engineering, particularly in the cut-and-thrust of competitive tendering for railway contracts, in which the ultimate performance is all-important for one's future business, I always view locomotive history with an eye to the end product—in other words, the capacity of a locomotive as a revenue-earning traffic unit.

In such a group as the Great Western standard gauge 4-4-0s one has, to use an artistic expression, an immense canvas upon which to work: the ceaseless interplay of fascinating mechanical details of construction, the glitter of copper-capped chimneys, polished brass safety-valve covers and other elegant touches, the West Country lore embodied in so many of the names, intertwined with searching questions as to why

One of the first batch of Dukes, No 3261 *Mount Edgcumbe,* built September 1895. *(British Railways)*

the Atbaras and the Cities were so exceptionally swift, why the Counties were so rough, and why Churchward perpetuated the double-frame design so long. Then again the case histories of some of the locomotives are unbelievably complicated in the saga of different boilers they carried, how their frames were modified, and so on. In a study like this, however, it is important to discern which are the changes that were purely matters of Works convenience, arising from the ready interchangeability of major components, and which were of real significance in respect to design and performance in their broadest aspects. So my own presentation of case histories at the end of the second volume is a record of broad outlines, rather than a minute documentation of every change.

The preparation of these two volumes has been a delightful task for me, not least in the personal memories that they have aroused. These locomotives were among the very first of which I became aware, now more than sixty-five years ago. I used to see Atbaras and Cities come flying through Reading on the Worcester expresses; holidays at Weymouth gave opportunities to see many Bulldogs and the occasional County, and it was at Weymouth that my father purchased for me my very first scale model locomotive—none other than a Gauge 1 Bassett-Lowke Atbara No 3410 *Sydney*. In later years I logged many runs, and made the occasional footplate trip, but for most of the performance data on which my assessment of the ultimate quality of these locomotives is made, I am dependent upon the records of the late A. V. Goodyear, and E. L. Bell, in addition of course to the writings of Charles Rous-Marten, in *The Engineer*, and in the early volumes of *The Railway Magazine*. I am especially indebted to

the Reverend Hilary Dunn in making available to me the log books compiled by his father, the Reverend W. A. Dunn, while he was in Bath during the early years of this century, and which contain a wealth of carefully compiled records of the working of these locomotives. The inside-cylinder engines were passing from the scene when Cecil J. Allen began his lengthy run of articles in *The Railway Magazine*, but searching the highways and hedges of railway literature I have been able to accumulate sufficient data to place these fascinating machines firmly on the map, quite apart from an epic like that of *City of Truro* on 9 May 1904.

This first volume takes the story up to the introduction of the last groups of inside-cylinder locomotives, before the place of the 4-4-0s in Churchward's master standardisation plan was fully evident. Chronologically one could place the concluding date as 1909, with the outside-cylindered Counties not yet having a mention, but I have included two outstanding runs by engines of the inside-cylinder type made over the new route to Birmingham, opened in 1910, which between them show work of the highest quality.

In addition to those who have, over many years, provided me with details of the running of these engines, I must express my indebtedness to many friends formerly in the service of the Great Western Railway who have 'filled me in' as the saying goes, with inside information. My gratitude is due to them all.

O. S. NOCK

Silver Cedars,
High Bannerdown,
Batheaston,
Bath.   *April 1977*

CHAPTER ONE

1894—A FALSE START

The last years of the broad gauge were difficult ones for the locomotive department of the Great Western Railway. Although the purely broad gauge services had been finally whittled down to the through expresses between London and the West of England, and local trains in Devon and Cornwall, on the appointed day for the final conversion twenty-seven first line express passenger engines would be made redundant overnight, together with the numerous tank engines of the 4-4-0 type used west of Newton Abbot. William Dean organised a number of improvisations, temporarily converting some of his standard gauge double-framed 0-6-0s into broad gauge, and building some of his new standard gauge 2-2-2 express engines as convertibles. The early history of these latter has a very important bearing upon the development of the 4-4-0s that are the subject of this book, and more than a passing reference to them is needed, by way of introduction.

Prior to 1892 Dean had not constructed an express passenger bogie engine. Like his great contemporary at Crewe he had remained out of step with the general trend of locomotive development in Great Britain in this respect, and his new standard express type of 1891, the 3001 class of 2-2-2 was in keeping with this tradition. It was a remarkable design. The cylinders, for example, had the largest diameter, 20in, ever put on to a British single-wheeler, while the boiler was notably large, with a total heating surface of 1466.73sq ft. To provide appropriate adhesion to match the high nominal tractive effort, the weight distribution was 13 tons 4 cwt on the leading wheels, 19 tons on the driving axle, and 12 tons on the trailer. This distribution led to a certain amount of fore-and-aft pitching with the driving axle as pivot, with repercussions to be described later. It is perhaps no more than incidental to the present theme

One of the 1892 batch of 7ft 8in singles built as 2-2-2 No 3009 *Flying Dutchman. (British Railways)*

9

One of the 7ft 8in singles built 1891 as a broad gauge convertible 2-2-2; here seen as rebuilt 1894 with Dean bogie. *(P. J. T. Reed)*

that eight of them were built as 'convertibles', and ran considerable mileage on the broad gauge before May 1892.

It is extraordinary how the mystique of William Stroudley pervaded British locomotive practice in the nineteenth century. One can understand how it influenced the Drummond brothers, and their successors on some of the Scottish railways, but it was strange to find it entering into an establishment of such strong individualism as Swindon. Yet before this particular story is finished, it will be seen that not only Stroudley, but quite foreign influences from both the USA and France, were to leave an indelible mark on Great Western practice. If ever an English engineer deserved the name of 'master mechanic'—not in the American, but in the literal sense—it was Stroudley; his arrangement of the slide valves beneath the cylinders, with direct actuation by Stephenson's link motion, was a case in point. It was a beautiful piece of mechanism, albeit somewhat inaccessible from the maintenance point of view. The first engineer to adopt it outside the LBSCR was James Holden who, from Carriage Assistant to Dean at Swindon had been appointed Locomotive Superintendent of the Great Eastern Railway. Dean himself adopted it in 1886 on the 7ft 8in 2-2-2 No 10. Until then nearly all Dean's locomotives, passenger and goods, had 17in by 24in cylinders, and the slide valves were

accommodated vertically, between the cylinders and driven directly by the link motion. It was the advance to 18in diameter cylinders, on the 2-2-2 No 10 that led Dean to adopt Stroudley's layout of the valves and motion.

Now with an engine over a pit it was simple enough to get to those underslung valves on a 2-2-2 with no obstruction other than the leading axle, but when the unsatisfactory riding of the 3001 class culminated in the derailment of No 3021 at full speed in the middle of Box Tunnel in 1893, something had to be done about it, and the straight answer was to substitute a leading bogie for the single leading axle. There were many bogie express locomotives running in Great Britain at that time, both of the 4-2-2 and of the 4-4-0 type, some having a truly enviable reputation for hard and reliable service, but none of these had Stroudley's arrangement of the valves. To provide a central pivot of the orthodox kind would make it extremely difficult to get to the slide valves. Bogies of an unconventional type had already been tried on individual Great Western engines, with notably unsuccessful results, and so for the 3001 class an entirely new design was worked out. As this design was unusual, and was applied to a large majority of the standard gauge 4-4-0s as well it requires detailed description.

Dean had designed a centre-less bogie that had been applied to coaching stock, and this new locomotive bogie was to some extent derived from this. Four downward projecting pillars were fixed to the inside frames, pitched with their centres about 6in fore and aft of where the bogie 'centre' was required to be. Then each pair of pillars, one on each of the frames, was connected by a massive transverse member between which, on the centre line of the locomotive was fixed a central block containing the bearing for the bogie pin. The bogie frames, which had outside bearings for the wheels, had transverse stretchers which were set downwards at the centre and were connected by the block that incorporated the inverted bogie pin. The cross-members connecting the pillars extending downwards from the main frames were themselves extended transversely, and from them long suspension bolts passed upwards to attachments on the bogie frame. It was through these four suspension bolts that the weight of the locomotive was transferred on to the bogie frame. To gain access to the covers of the valve chests, the ornamental nuts at the base of the four pillars were first removed. When the front end of the locomotive was lifted so that the bottom of the suspension bolts cleared the bogie attachment, the bogie itself could be run clear. With only the main frame cross-members remaining, together with the bogie bearing block, access to the valves was comparatively easy from a pit.

This, then, was the bogie that was eventually fitted to all except the last thirty-five double-framed inside cylindered 4-4-0s of the Great Western Railway, in addition of course to the eighty 4-2-2s of the 3001 class, proving to be an extremely effective and reliable design. It was this bogie that guided *City of Truro* round the long sweeping curves of the Wellington bank in its meteoric dash down from Whiteball Tunnel on 9 May 1904, but more significantly perhaps in the marvellous running over the much sharper curves of the South Devon line, over which it performed, surely, at the very limit of safety. The guiding influence on that bogie was the contact between the centre pin and bearing, where there was a small amount of side play and the side springs. I shall describe later in this book how this bogie was superseded on the last batches of both the 6ft 8in and 5ft 8in inside-cylinder 4-4-0s, and how all the older locomotives of the series came to have the newer form of bogie. The original type could readily be recognised by the large polished nuts at the bottom ends of the suspension bolts, which could be seen projecting below the frames of the bogie itself. The washers had spherical seatings and the suspension bolts themselves were in the nature of swing links, though permitting very little side play. The bogies were richly ornamented. The caps on the spring hangers

First of the 7ft 0in 4-4-0s, No 7 *Armstrong*, at Bristol Temple Meads. *(L & GRP)*

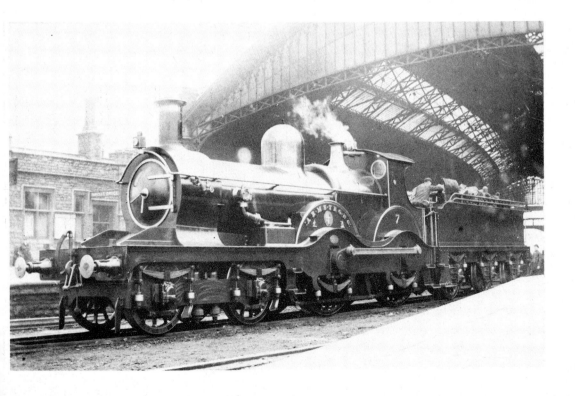

were polished bright, while the wheel splashers—another refinement—had polished brass edgings.

The other feature of the 3001 class that was inherited by the subsequent 4-4-0s was the setting as well as the arrangement of the valve gear. When James Holden copied Stroudley's layout of the Stephenson link motion he gave the valves a maximum travel of no more than 3⅞in in full gear. Dean increased this to 4⅝in and this feature, combined with generous port openings when the gear was partly linked-up, was a factor that helped to make all the Dean express engines the very fast machines they were. So much, then, by way of preliminaries. We can now pass on to the 4-4-0s themselves.

At the end of the year 1893 Swindon had on its hands three 2-4-0 convertibles that had lain idle since the final liquidation of the broad gauge. Two of these were two-cylinder simples, and the third was a four-cylinder tandem compound. They had the running numbers 14, 16 and 8 respectively. There was a fourth 7ft 2-4-0 No 7, also a tandem compound, but built for the standard gauge. Like the convertible No 8 it was not successful, and did very little work. When the time came for converting Nos 8, 14 and 16 to standard gauge the troubles with the 3001 class 2-2-2s had reached such a stage that Dean decided to rebuild these 2-4-0s as 4-4-0s, though so complete was the metamorphosis that 'replacement' would be a truer description of what happened. Little except the

wheel centres can have been used. The standard gauge compound 2-4-0 No 7 was also included in this operation. So in 1894 came the first standard gauge express passenger 4-4-0s on the GWR. The four locomotives were named, in order *Armstrong, Gooch, Charles Saunders,* and *Brunel.*

They could broadly be described as a 4-4-0 version of the 3001 class 7ft 8in 4-2-2s, having interchangeable boilers, the Stroudley arrangement of valves and valve gear, and the suspension type of bogie. But the cylinders were even larger, 20in diameter by 26in stroke. The cylinder volume was considerably the largest then provided on a British 4-4-0, and it is interesting to compare the proportions, in relation to heating surface, with those of other large and powerful designs then giving satisfactory service. All these had 7ft 0in diameter coupled wheels and mostly 19in by 26in cylinders. I have picked out three famous and successful classes that were established by the time Dean's Armstrong class took the road.

Four 7ft 0in 4—4—0 Designs

Railway	Designer	Cylinders dia in	stroke in	Total heating surface sq ft	Boiler Pressure lb/sq in
Midland	S.W.Johnson	18 1/2	26	1223	160
LSWR	W.Adams	19	26	1367	175
North Eastern	W.Worsdell	19	26	1341	180
GWR	W.Dean	20	26	1561.3	160

With a certain amount of hindsight the Armstrongs have been criticised as over-cylindered, but in relation to the total heating surface this was not so. They were built at a time

4-4-0 No 14 *Charles Saunders*; the first locomotive on which Sir William Stanier worked as an apprentice. *(British Railways)*

2-4-0 No 69 *Avon,* on which Dean used the Stroudley method of balancing. *(O. S. Nock collection)*

when British engineers were deliberately providing cylinder volumes that were large in relation to boiler capacity to ensure that locomotives were driven at economical rates of expansion. It was impossible to thrash them without running short of steam. Adams' LSWR 4-4-0s were habitually driven at cut-offs of less than 20 per cent.

In the design of the Armstrongs Dean adopted another feature of Stroudley's practice —rather curiously too. With inside-cylindered locomotives it was the normal practice to set the crankpin for the coupling rod diametrically opposite to the main driving crankpin on which the big-end was mounted. This arrangement gave a degree of natural balance between the revolving parts, but Stroudley put the inside and outside crankpins in line. His reason for doing this was explained in his celebrated paper to the Institution of Civil Engineers in 1885. He told then how in his earlier experiences with outside-cylindered locomotives on the Highland Railway that the axleboxes, brasses, horn blocks and connecting rods of those locomotives lasted roughly twice as long as those of comparable inside-cylinder locomotives. One is a little curious to know what these 'comparable' locomotives were, because his previous experi- ence had been in the running sheds of the Great Northern at Peterborough in Sturrock's time, and after he left the Highland he took over Craven's bequests to the Brighton. He formed the opinion that the superiority of performance of the outside-cylinder locomotives was because the coupling rod and connecting rod were placed on the same side of the axle, using the same crankpin. He claimed there was uniformity of

movement, the coupling rods taking up the strain smoothly, whereas with a conventional inside-cylinder locomotive the cranks, and with them the stresses, were in opposition. Few of his contemporaries agreed with Stroudley on this, and the heavy balance weights he had to put in the wheels caused a surging motion when the locomotives were running, which caused one class that was particularly bad to be nicknamed the 'seasick engines'. Dean liked Stroudley's arrangement, and fitted it when he rebuilt eight of the 2-2-2 singles as outside-framed 2-4-0s, and named them after rivers.

Whichever way Stroudley might argue, his design of crank axle necessitated the inclusion of heavy crescent-shaped balance weights in the wheels. It not only made the complete driving axle assembly—wheels and crank axle—very awkward to wheel around in the shops, but resulted in a heavy hammer-blow effect on the rails when the locomotive was running at speed. Of course express train speeds on the Brighton line were not very high in Stroudley's time, rarely much over 60mph and the hammer-blow was less pronounced than at 75 or 80mph. With an outside-cylindered engine like the Adams 4-4-0s of the LSWR, and Churchward's County class, discussed in the second volume of this book, there is only one crankpin on each side, common to both the connecting and coupling rod; while there is thus a certain measure of the same unbalancing effect, the driving axle between the frames is straight, and without the massive sheaves carrying the crankpins of an

A broadside view of No 8 *Gooch,* emphasising its beautiful proportions. *(L & GRP)*

inside-cylindered engine.

I have referred to the building of these four locomotives as a false start, and so it was technically in the light of subsequent development of the 4-4-0 type on the Great Western Railway. Aesthetically and artistically, however, they were the ultimate glory of nineteenth century elegance—by some regarded as more beautiful engines even than the 7ft 8in 4-2-2s of the 3001 class. They were an embodiment of the fascinating old time lore of the Great Western before the regimentation of standards took everything in its grip, even to the systematic numbering. There was something individual about their very numbers 7, 8, 14 and 16, not in any grouped sequence. At a time when the broad gauge was gone, and everyone on the line was looking forward to a time of great expansion, and a revival of the spirit of boundless enterprise in which the railway had been born sixty years

4-4-0 No 16 *Brunel,* with its third type of boiler: three-quarter coned, as from 1909. *(British Railways)*

earlier, the great men of the past were not forgotten. With Brunel, Gooch and Saunders was coupled the name of the 'clan' that served the line for so long, in both broad and standard gauge days, and which gave its name to this small, but distinguished class of locomotives.

Gifted artists of our own time have striven to recapture something of the crowning elegance of these engines; the balanced symmetry of their lines, in the way the historic Brunswick green was blended with the crimson lake of their splashers, and underframes. When an attempt was made to revive the old Dean livery on *City of Truro* in 1957 the red was given a brownish hue, which enthusiasts with long memories immediately criticised. Reproductions of some of the famous F. Moore paintings may have given rise to this comparatively recent rendering; whatever colour the twentieth century 4-4-0s may have carried before Churchward superseded it by black there is no doubt that the Dean singles and the four Armstrongs had their splashers and underframes in a rich crimson lake. The names were carried in raised brass letters on the splashers, and the numbers in

large brass figures on the cab sides. The only criticism that one could make of their appearance was that they looked a little squat when seen from the photographer's usual stance at the lineside. Although they had the same boiler as the 3001 class, the smaller diameter of the driving wheels enabled it to be pitched 3½in lower. The chimney was made proportionately longer.

Few detailed records seem to have survived of the running of these four beautiful engines. In the early days of his apprenticeship at Swindon, No 14 *Charles Saunders* was the very first locomotive on which the late Sir William Stanier worked. In the many enjoyable talks I had with him when I was writing his biography I gathered that his principal interest in the locomotive was in its bogie, and the setting of its slide valves, rather than of any subsequent work out on the road. The class worked mainly between Paddington and Bristol at a time when the 7ft 8in singles of the 3001 class had all the limelight to themselves. But in view of the large cylinder volume on both the singles and on the Armstrongs it is perhaps significant that both classes had their cylinder diameter reduced from 20in to 19in. It is perhaps anticipating history a little to tell how these four locomotives fared under the Churchward standardisation programme, but the interesting point is that 'odd men out' as they were they were not scrapped, and their elegant frames were embodied in the building-up of engines that

were new in everything except the frames, the names, and the leading bogies.

For a time No 14 was working on the 10.45am South Wales express, which then ran via Bath and Bristol Stapleton Road. The locomotive worked the train as far as Newport, returning by the train due in Paddington at 6.40pm. The down train was allowed the level two hours to Bath, and when Rous-Marten travelled by it, the engine lost nearly 5 minutes net on this moderate schedule. An abbreviated log is shown below. Neither permanent way check was severe, and although the load was no more than 150 tons the speed was mediocre. No higher maximum was attained than 67mph down either the Dauntsey or the Box Tunnel inclines. The up train had the generous allowance of 135 minutes non-stop from Bath to Paddington, and despite two permanent way checks and a signal stop, this timing was practically kept. But it was not a very inspiring performance. From what Rous-Marten wrote at the time it seemed typical of the Armstrongs. One can only guess at what made them so sluggish compared particularly to the Badmintons that followed, which were very fast engines. One can only think that there must have been some misjudgment in the proportioning of their port openings and steam passages that led to a restriction in the flow of steam. We know from the history of many other locomotives—not Great Western—what an extraordinarily hampering effect such restrictions can have.

GWR 10.45am PADDINGTON-BATH
Locomotive No 14 *Charles Saunders*
Load 150 tons

Distance Miles		Actual min secs	Average speed mph
0.0	Paddington	0 00	—
—		pws	—
18.5	Slough	25 10	44.0
36.0	Reading	44 58	53.3
53.1	Didcot	63 49	54.4
77.3	Swindon	92 28	50.7
—		pws	—
94.0	Chippenham	112 26	50.0
106.9	Bath	127 46	50.7

GWR 4.25pm BATH-PADDINGTON
Locomotive No 14 *Charles Saunders*
Load 170 tons

Distance Miles		Actual min secs	Average speed mph
0.0	Bath	0 00	—
—		pws	—
12.9	Chippenham	21 01	—
—		pws	—
29.6	Swindon	43 38	—
—		signal stop	—
53.8	Didcot	73 54	—
70.9	Reading	94 33	49.5
88.4	Slough	113 34	55.2
106.9	Paddington	135 28	50.7

(Details of the subsequent rebuilding of these four locomotives are given on page 94).

CHAPTER TWO

DUKE CLASS—THE 5ft 8in SAGA BEGINS

Throughout broad gauge days Newton Abbot was a major divisional point in the locomotive working. Although Exeter was the easternmost extent of the South Devon Railway the famous eight-foot 4-2-2s worked through between Bristol and Newton Abbot, and the whole service beyond the latter point was worked by the various classes of 4-4-0 saddle tanks. When the change came to the standard gauge the Dean 4-2-2s of the 3001 class became the regular engines east of Newton Abbot, and a new type altogether was designed for the heavy gradients of the West Country. The first of the new type, appropriately named *Duke of Cornwall,* was completed at Swindon in 1895. In the light of what had gone before it had some unusual and unexpected features. It was the last Great Western passenger locomotive design that could be described as pure Dean, and in view of the

King Arthur as originally built in 1895. The name was removed in 1927 to avoid 'confusion' with other locomotives named after Kings! *(British Railways)*

heavy uphill work that was required in the West Country it might at first sight have seemed strange that having used 20in diameter cylinders on his high-speed 4-2-2 and 4-4-0 engines there should have been a reversion to 18in on the Dukes. It is probable, however, that some considerable restriction in axle loading was imposed over Brunel's timber trestle viaducts. In any case the boiler was much smaller than that of the earlier eight-wheeled tender engines, having a total heating surface of 1398.18sq ft against 1561.33sq ft on the Armstrongs, and the maximum axle load was 15.35 tons, against 15.9 tons. The load on the bogie was 17.5 tons against 19.3 tons.

The boiler was one by itself in the range of inside cylinder 4-4-0s covered by the present study, in having a flush round-topped firebox, and a huge extended smokebox. It is strange that Dean should have abandoned, in one of his last designs, the form of firebox with the top raised above the level of the boiler barrel, because the feature was so advantageous in

providing additional steam space above the water line, thus minimising any tendency to prime. But with such an enormous dome the provision of extra steam space above the crown of the firebox was evidently thought to be unnecessary. The huge, and aggressive-looking extended smokebox was to provide for a diaphragm plate and netting for spark arresting, and could be discerned as the very first evidence of Churchward's influence in locomotive design at Swindon. At the time the first Dukes were built in 1895 Churchward was manager of the carriage works, but his keen interest in locomotive work and his familiarity with current practice in the USA suggest that the adoption of so characteristic a feature of American practice as the long extended smokebox and the diaphragm plate was probably made at his instigation.

Another striking feature of the first batches of the Duke class was the use of Mansell pattern wood-centred coach wheels for the engine bogie and for the tender. The first forty engines and the first twenty-five tenders were so equipped. The tenders were extremely short, having a wheel-base of no more than 11ft 0in. It must be recalled, however, that prior to the abolition of the broad gauge the line west of Newton Abbot had been worked exclusively by tank engines, and the turntables were appropriately short. Even with their very short tenders something of a contortionist act was necessary at some sheds to turn the Duke class. The tenders had to be

jacked up, because their rear ends extended beyond the length of the turntable, and the rearmost wheels lifted clear of the rails.

The Dukes, which in their early days were also known variously as the Pendennis Castle class, and also as the Devons had a long and diverse career, involving many changes of boiler. These began after the first forty of the class had been built, up to March 1897. These first batches had charming names, nearly all connected with the lore, history and legends of the West Country. Although there was 'system' in their naming there was none of the interminable tedium of the systematised class naming that imposed a positive stranglehold on Great Western locomotive nomenclature from the 1930s onwards. The first forty Dukes contained in their names a happy mixture of geography, personalities, legends, and even West Country saints, with which latter there was no confusion with Churchward's 2900 class 4-6-0s. In Swindon terminology, *St. Agnes, St. Anthony, St. Germans,* and *St. Michael* would never have been regarded as Saints any more than *Sir Lancelot* would have been confused with the Knights. Then look at such lovely names as *Armorel, Chough* and *Tre Pol and Pen,* and it can be realised with what good taste and artistic feeling the titles were chosen. Even the geographical ones like *Eddystone, Tintagel* and

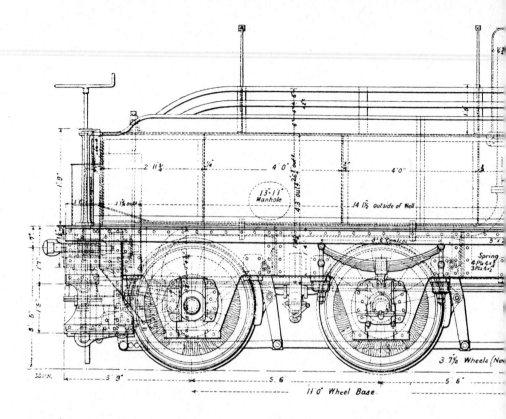

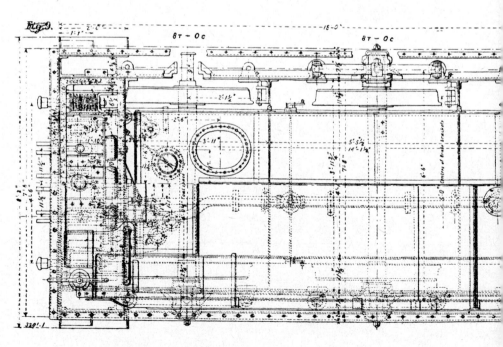

The short wheelbase original tender of the Duke class
locomotive, showing the wooden 'spoked' wheels.

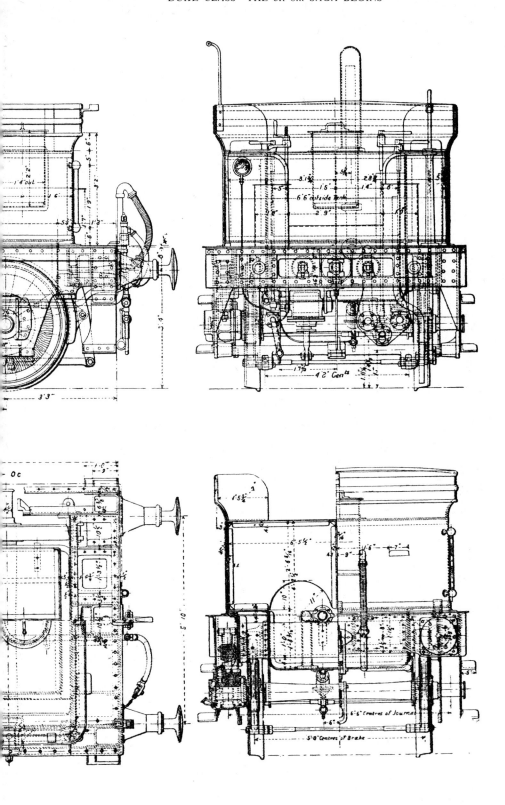

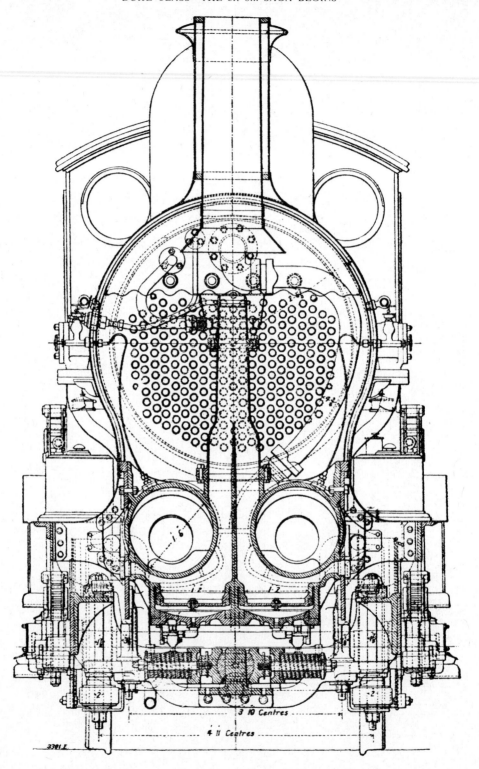

Cross-section at smokebox and cylinders.

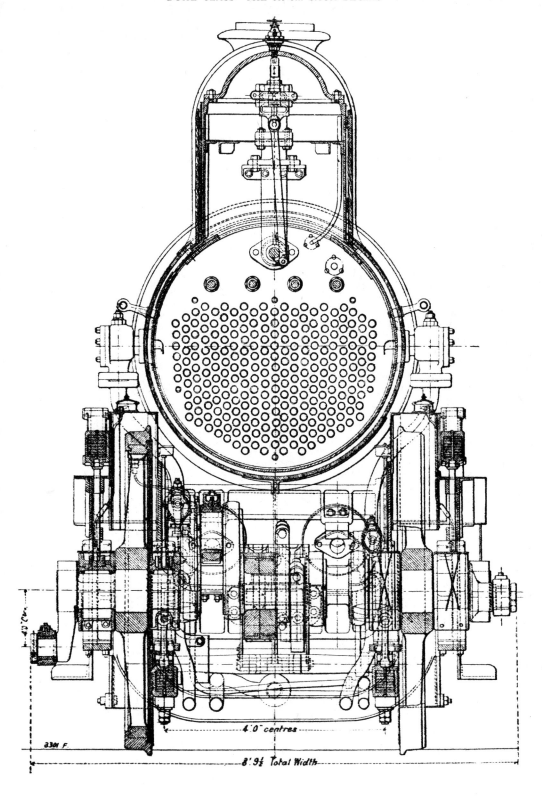

Cross-section showing crank axle, dome, regulator, and arrangement of tubes.

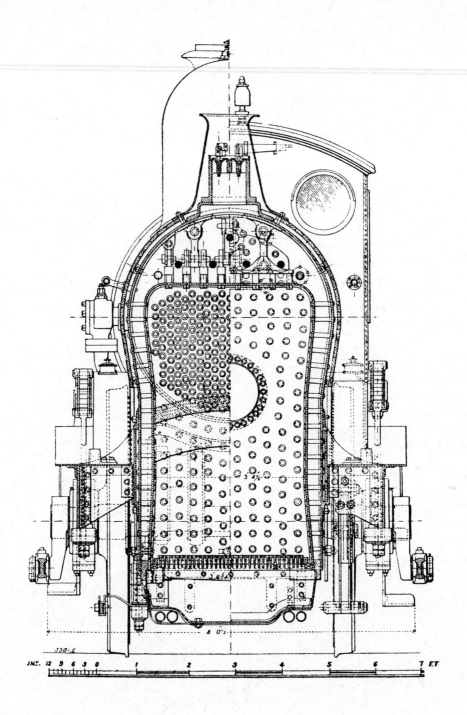

Cross-section through firebox.

Cab view, showing extreme simplicity of the fittings.

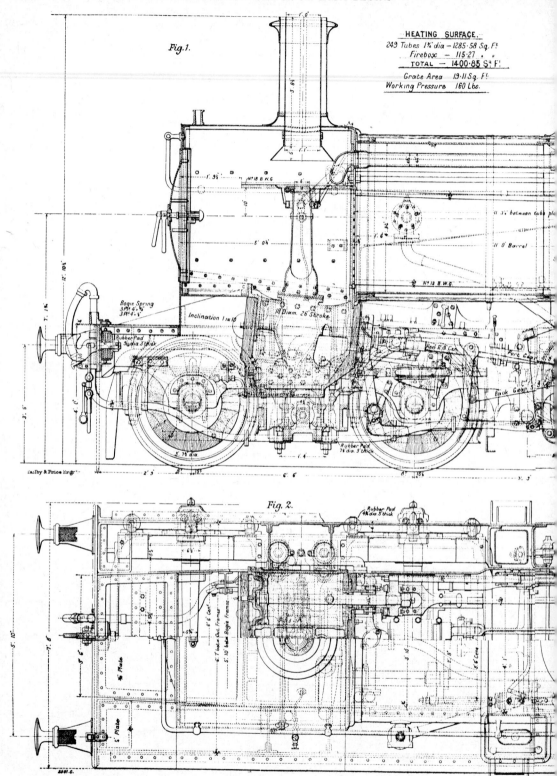

Fig.1.

HEATING SURFACE.
249 Tubes 1¾ dia — 1285·58 Sq. Ft
Fireboxo — 115·27 "
TOTAL — 1400·85 Sq Ft
Grate Area 19·11 Sq. Ft
Working Pressure 160 Lbs.

Fig. 2.

Sectional elevation and plan of Duke class locomotive
as originally built.

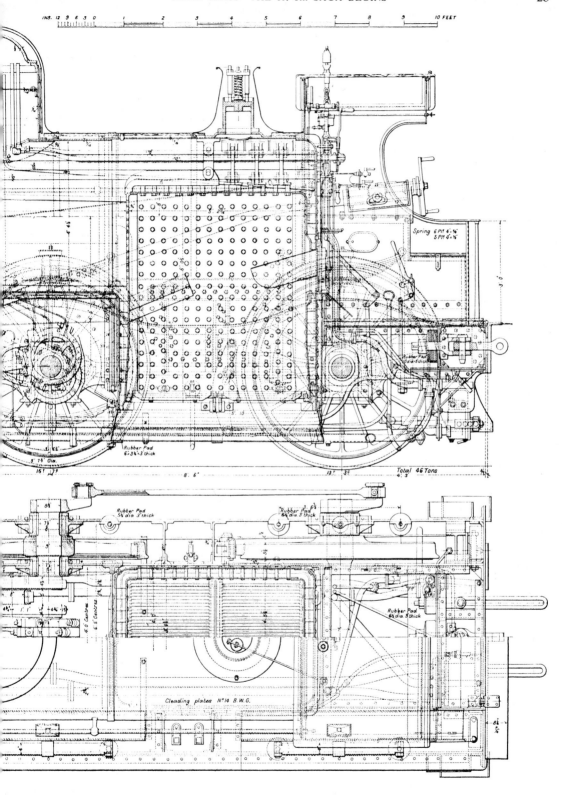

Duke No 3270 *Trevithick* in running colours. *(British Railways)*

Mounts Bay had none of the adherence to 'system' that sometimes made ridiculous the same technique, used elsewhere with less imagination—*Portland Bill* for example!

DUKE CLASS DIMENSIONS

Cylinders, dia. 18in
    stroke 26in
Boiler, barrel,
    length 11ft 0in
    distance between
    tube plates 11ft 3 1/4in
Smokebox, length 5ft 0 7/8in
Firebox, length 5ft 10in
Heating surfaces:
    Tubes   1285.58sq ft
    Firebox   115.27sq ft
Grate Area   19.11sq ft
Boiler pressure, 160lb per sq in
Adhesion weight, 28 1/2 tons
Total engine weight 46 tons
Total tender weight 24 tons
Nominal tractive effort
    at 85% boiler press, 17,000lb

The boiler was an excellent steam-raiser. The deep-set narrow firebox was easy to fire, the tubes were of large diameter in relation to their length, and from the detail drawings it will be seen how simple and direct were the passages from the exhaust ports to the blastpipe, the cap of which had a diameter of no less than 5in. A feature that was a little curious by later practice was that there was no definite choke in the chimney—in fact the diameter at the base, 1ft 1in, was actually larger than that at the top, 1ft 0in. It is evident that the chimney was proportioned so that the cone of exhaust steam from the blastpipe cap just filled the chimney at the top. The cross-sectional drawing on page 22 shows how far the spark-arresting netting extended forward of the blastpipe. Taken all

round one gains the impression of an excellently-designed well-balanced locomotive, ideal for the heavy intermittent work of the West Country.

Until the introduction of the Dukes, Great Western locomotives had carried their names on the driving wheel splashers, in cast raised letters on a plate of appropriate radius. But on the Dukes the smaller diameter of coupled wheel and the use of overhung springs left no room in the traditional place, especially as many of the new names were long, so horizontal plates were fitted extending forward from the boiler band central with the dome, to a point just in the rear of the large clack boxes of the boiler feed. These plates were made the same length irrespective of the length of the name, so that while *Duke of Cornwall* had the letters neatly and compactly spaced, names like *Amyas, Chough,* or *Merlin* were strung out to fill the plate. The number-plates were placed high on the cab sides in line with the nameplates.

The elaboration of the finish can be appreciated from the broadside official photograph of *Duke of Cornwall*, and with the frames in crimson lake, the double lining-out of the boiler bands, and the profusion of polished detail work, on the bogies, spring hangers and clack boxes, quite apart from tremendous features like that dome, the overall effect was to make them extraordinarily impressive engines, small though they were. Because of the shortness of the tenders the usual Great Western painting style with three panels was not used, and the elaborately intertwined scroll letters GWR were set in the middle of a single panel. In passing, one could hardly imagine a detail more typical of the Victorian era of railways, and especially of the Great Western, than that scroll. It did not take Churchward very long to discard it. The cab fittings could not be simpler, though the shelter itself was narrow, to give plenty of room within the structure gauge for an engineman to climb out along the running plate when necessary. Dean used only a single water gauge glass, a feature followed in all Great Western engines through Churchward's, Collett's and Hawksworth's days.

THE FIRST FORTY DUKES

Original Number	Name	Built
3252	Duke of Cornwall	1895
3253	Pendennis Castle	,,
3254	Boscawen	,,
3255	Cornubia	,,
3256	Excalibur	,,
3257	Guinevere	,,
3258	King Arthur	,,
3259	Lizard	,,
3260	Merlin	,,
3261	Mount Edgcumbe	,,
3262	Powderham	1896
3263	Sir Lancelot	,,
3264	St. Anthony	,,
3265	St. Germans	,,
3266	St. Ives	,,
3267	St. Michael	,,
3268	Tamar	,,
3269	Tintagel	,,
3270	Trevithick	,,
3271	Tre Pol and Pen	,,
3272	Amyas	,,
3273	Armorel	,,
3274	Cornishman	,,
3275	Chough	,,
3276	Dartmoor	,,
3277	Earl of Devon	1897
3278	Eddystone	,,
3279	Exmoor	,,
3280	Falmouth	,,
3281	Fowey	,,
3282	Maristow	,,
3283	Mounts Bay	,,
3284	Newquay	,,
3285	St. Erth	,,
3286	St. Just	,,
3287	St. Agnes	,,
3288	Tresco	,,
3289	Trefusis	,,
3290	Torbay	,,
3291	Tregenna	,,

The detail design of the 'Dukes' can be studied from the working drawings reproduced on pages 20, 21, 22, 24, and 25, while the arrangement of the very short wheelbased tender is shown on pages 18 and 19. The tender wheels and the engine bogie wheels were alike and of the same diameter, being of the Mansell coach pattern, while the construction of the Dean type bogie can be seen from the side elevation view, page 24, and the cross section at the cylinders on page 20. These engines did not have the Stroudley arrangement of driving cranks and coupling crankpins, because these were placed in the more conventional position, diametrically opposite, as can be seen from the cross-sectioned view on page 21. The slide valves were positioned underneath, in the Stroudley style, in keeping with the arrangement that was standardised on all Great Western engines with inside cylinders 18in diameter and upwards. The actual valve dimensions were the same as those of the Armstrongs.

With the introduction of the Duke class in 1895 certain changes were made in the locomotive workings in South Devon and Cornwall. The smaller coupled wheels and rapid accelerative capacity of the new engines was found to be of considerable advantage on the coastal part of the South Devon line, between Exeter and Newton Abbot. Although the line is level throughout it was then far from a high-speed stretch. The trains had to be accelerated from dead slow running at either end, and intermediately there was the section of single line along the sea wall between Dawlish and Teignmouth, with severe slowings for single-line token collecting and discharging at the two ends. Despite the absence of gradients single-wheelers were not ideal for such a line, and on many of the important trains it became the practice to change engines at Exeter rather than at Newton Abbot. On one portion of the Cornishman one engine worked through between Exeter and Falmouth.

Late in 1895 Duke class locomotives took an important part in the working of the very first Ocean Mail specials run by the GWR, long before the exciting competition with the LSWR began. The first of these specials was run on Thursday 28 November, leaving the dockside, Millbay, at 7.00am. The train consisted of five vehicles: two eight-wheeled and one six-wheeled van, plus one six-wheeled, and one eight-wheeled saloon, having together a tare weight of 121 tons. The gross load was probably about 130 tons, and as far as Exeter it was worked by No 3256 Excalibur. As on the famous runs of 1904 a stop had to be made at the dock gates to attach the main line engine, and from there the train ran non-stop to Exeter. This run, and that made three weeks later, can be considered together. On the latter the tare load of the train was 115 tons, with the pioneer engine of the class

No 3252 *Duke of Cornwall*. Summary details of the two runs were:

Distance Miles		No 3256 121 tons tare		No 3252 115 tons tare	
		Time min	Av. speed mph	Time min	Av. speed mph
	Millbay Dock				
0.0	Gates	0	—	0	—
32.7	Newton Abbot	44 1/2	44.05	44	44.5
52.9	Exeter	68	51.43	66	55.0

When it is considered that not until 30 April 1904, with the 'Race from the West' working up to its climax, was the time from Millbay to Exeter brought below sixty-six minutes, and with comparable loads, the above performances stand out as remarkable.

Subsequent to the above runs Charles Rous-Marten made a number of journeys west of Plymouth, but tantalisingly gives little actual detail. He travelled with Dukes, the domeless-boilered Camels and the 3521 class, of which more anon, and had this to say, in general:

All did very satisfactory work, but as the entire Cornish system is a series of sharp reverse curves and excessively severe grades,

often 1 in 50 to 1 in 60, it is obvious that the work is necessarily of a plodding or 'hard-slogging' nature, very useful, but not attractive to the general reader in respect of detail. The doughty small-wheeled engines showed some excellent pulling up the steep banks, but owing to the sharpness of the curves they were debarred from attaining any really high speeds on the descending grades. As a rule they ran down the steep hills with steam off and a frequent touch of the brake. They were rarely allowed to exceed a maximum of 50 to 55 miles an hour. Nor, in view of the strong lateral movement often experienced at the tail end of the train in turning the numerous sharp curves, can this precaution be deemed other than prudent. There is nothing else in all Britain that equals, if it approach, the Great Western line from Exeter to Falmouth and Penzance in respect of excessive difficulty as an express route, and whatever further accelerations we may see, as I have no doubt we shall, at no distant date, between Paddington and Exeter, I fear we can hardly look for an average inclusive speed very greatly in excess of 30 miles an hour west of Newton Abbot. The doubling of the Parson Tunnels and of the remaining lengths of single line in Cornwall will no doubt make some difference, and several of the worst

A right-hand side view of No 3289 *Trefusis*, emphasising the massive appearance. *(O. S. Nock collection)*

No 3275 *Chough*, built in November 1896, but here shown with later type of nameplate, tender with side fenders, and later standard inscription. *(H. W. Burman)*

curves are being improved; but I do not see how the South Devon and Cornwall sections can ever cease to be in a separate category from the rest of the Great Western system, and indeed from all other British railways, not even excepting the Highland.

The details of a journey, compiled by Rous-Marten does not include any notes of the minimum speeds up the Hemerdon and Dainton inclines; but comparing the times with some of my own runs, I should guess that they were about 15mph up Hemerdon bank, and 18mph at Dainton. The general standard of performance was much the same as that which prevailed in the 1920s, with the larger loads appropriate to the 4-6-0 locomotives then in use.

From the year 1896 onwards it is difficult to keep developments in Great Western locomotive practice in their strictly chronological order. The increasing influence of Churchward, which came about in the manner described in the next chapter, could be seen in certain locomotives in the final batch of Dukes built at Swindon in 1899. Fifteen of these were standard with those that had gone previously, except that Mansell-pattern wheels were not used. The last four had a moderately raised Belpaire firebox, while the first, which actually preceded the standard engines by five months, was the celebrated *Bulldog*. Thus by August 1899 there were fifty-five standard Dukes with flush round-topped fireboxes, four with Churchward developments in the form of raised Belpaire fireboxes, and one with a much larger boiler. Twenty engines including the last named were subsequently transferred to the later Bulldog class, and at this

stage I am concerned only with the forty remaining engines of the Duke class proper, which had a long and notable history.

First then, to boiler changes. With the large dome on the back ring of the boiler there was not the need for a high raised firebox to provide additional steam space above the water line, and in November 1903 *Comet* was fitted with a flush-topped Belpaire firebox. This proved to be the standard equipment for the latter part of the lives of these locomotives, not changing in outward appearance when, at a later date, superheaters were added. The reboilering was very gradual, and up to the end of the year 1910 only eighteen engines had been treated. Not all those had the flush-topped Belpaire type. Seven of them, *St. Michael, Dartmoor, Earl of Devon, Trefusis, Tregenna, Severn,* and *Weymouth,* received domeless parallel boilers with raised Belpaire fireboxes, and three, *St. Ives, Eddystone* and *Cotswold* received this domeless type, after first receiving the flush-topped Belpaire type with domes. These permutations had no more significance than that of demonstrating the interchangeability of the various boilers then in current use on the GWR. Early in the Churchward regime the locomotives lost their gorgeous external finish, with the underframes black instead of crimson, and the domes painted green. They also received the new standard curved nameplates mounted above rather than on the splashers. With one exception the whole class of forty locomotives had the flush-topped

Belpaire firebox and large dome by May 1917. The exception was *Trefusis*, which retained a domeless boiler and raised Belpaire firebox until December 1923. Then after a spell with the standard boiler it reverted once again to the domeless type in April 1926, retaining it for another three years. The fitting of superheaters and piston valves is referred to in a later chapter.

The Dukes were very quickly superseded on the best trains in the West Country by the domeless-boilered Camels, and played a second-ary role for many years. That they did it very well is beyond any doubt; the later locomotives were not precluded from running over the timber trestle viaducts that remained on the Falmouth branch into the 1930s, and so the Dukes did not even have that line to themselves. When I first travelled into Cornwall in 1924, there were a few of them stationed at Newton Abbot and Laira for providing assistance on the South Devon banks, and there was at least one of them working from Truro on the Falmouth branch. It was a stirring sight, in the late 1920s to see a Duke piloting a King up the Dainton and Rattery inclines. Grouping brought a new lease of life to many of them, because their moderate axle loading enabled them to be drafted on to the Cambrian Line, where they immediately took over the principal passenger workings from the superannuated local 4-4-0s.

No 3289, the original 3326 of July 1899, featured in one of those amusing editorial bloomers that sometimes affect even the most reliable journals. It was shown double-heading one of the new four-cylinder 4-6-0s, No 5007 *Rougemont Castle*, west of Newton Abbot, and described as working a 'Paddington - Aller Junction train'! It reminded me of the Mystery Tour trains that once were run from Paddington, and made one speculate as to what the reactions would have been if a train load of passengers *had* been dumped down in the country near Aller Junction. There is in fact more point to the story than the muddle-headedness of a sub-editor, because the Duke class engine concerned was one of the twelve that had their names removed in 1930, because the Traffic Depart-ment feared that these might be a source of confusion to passengers, and indicate instead the destination of the train itself. While one could concede that there was some justification

in taking off *Falmouth*, *Newquay* and *Weymouth*, albeit after the engines had borne those names for more than thirty years, I always felt it was carrying things to extremes to take off those of the Cornish saints that also happened to be the names of stations: *St. Agnes*, *St. Columb*, *St. Austell*, *St. Erth*, and above all *St. Just*. It would be an optimistic passenger who expected to be taken by a through train to any of the several villages carrying that saint's name.

The subsequent technical history of these well-loved locomotives is covered in the sections dealing with superheating and top feed apparatus. Twenty-nine of them were replaced by the hybrid 3200 class from 1936 onwards, in addition to No 3265 *Tre Pol and Pen*, which in 1929 was rebuilt and became the 'guinea pig' of the 3200 class. It was the original intention that all the remaining Dukes should be replaced by 3200s, but this programme was not carried out, and nine Dukes survived. Although the comprehensive case histories are set out later, it is of interest to recall the names of the ten survivors, and the dates of their ultimate withdrawal:

1946 No	Pre-1946 No	Name	Withdrawn
9054	3254	*Cornubia*	June 1950
9064	3264	*Trevithick*	December 1949
9072	3272	formerly *Fowey*	June 1949
9073	3273	*Mounts Bay*	December 1949
9076	3276	formerly *St. Agnes*	November 1949
9083	3283	*Comet*	December 1950
9084	3284	*Isle of Jersey*	April 1951
9087	3287	*Mercury*	July 1949
9089	3289	formerly *St. Austell*	July 1951
9091	3291	*Thames*	February 1949

In addition to the above there was the rebuilt No 3265 (9065) *Tre Pol and Pen*, which was not withdrawn until December 1949. At one time it was intended to renumber that engine 3200, in the same way as the rebuilt 4-6-0 No 2925 *Saint Martin* became 4900, the prototype of the Halls, but this intention did not materialise and *Tre Pol and Pen* remained No 3265 until renumbered 9065 in 1946, under which number it was withdrawn. It will be seen that No 3289 the engine of the 'Paddington - Aller Junction mystery train' was the last to survive.

CHAPTER THREE

THE CHURCHWARD ENTRÉE—PHASE 1

In 1895 when the first of the Dukes was built at Swindon, Samuel Carlton was Locomotive Works Manager. He was one of those distinguished engineers who had joined the Great Western at Wolverhampton under Joseph Armstrong, following him to Swindon to become Works Manager, a post that he held for more than thirty years. In 1895 his assistant was a vigorous and brilliant young man named Douglas Earle Marsh. One of the changes on the Great Northern Railway following the deaths of

G. J. Churchward, Locomotive, Carriage and Wagon Superintendent from 1902. *(British Railways)*

Patrick Stirling and of his assistant Mr Shotton, left the Works Managership at Doncaster vacant, and to this Earle Marsh was appointed, taking office in January 1896. At Swindon G. J. Churchward, until then Manager of the Carriage Works, was appointed assistant to Mr Carlton in the Locomotive Works, but on 24 March 1896 Carlton died, and shortly afterwards Churchward was appointed to succeed him. F. J. Wright, who had been Chief Draughtsman became Assistant Locomotive Works Manager, and H. T. King was appointed Chief Draughtsman. A year later Churchward was appointed Assistant Locomotive, Carriage & Wagon Superintendent while retaining his existing appointment.

It was an unusual assignment, but the circumstances that led up to it were unusual, too. Those who have studied Great Western locomotive practice in any detail have remarked upon the evidences, particularly from 1898 onwards, of Churchward's influence while Dean remained in the chair. It might have been imagined that this was a pleasant case of a distinguished elder statesman of the engineering profession giving scope to a brilliant assistant to develop his own ideas, but this was unhappily not the case. It was, on the contrary, no more than a few outward and visible signs of a great human tragedy. By 1896 it was becoming evident to the Locomotive Committee of the Board, to whom he reported directly, that Dean's mental capacity was beginning to fail, and that the outstanding success with which he had managed his large department hitherto was likely to be seriously impaired. But he was still expecting to remain in office for a number of years, and the way the Board dealt with this difficult situation was a monument of kindly, psychological understanding of human nature. It would have been easy enough to have given him a 'golden handshake' and relieved him of all his duties, and the result in so difficult a case would have been bewilderment for Dean, bitterness, and an earlier end to his life. They were however supremely fortunate in having such a man as Churchward to put in as assistant, for quite apart from his ability as an engineer, Churchward had a warmly human side to his character, and for five years played the delicate part confided to him with consummate tact and unerring judgment.

That he did so well in handling the great human problem put to him was in large measure due to the nature of his own genius as an engineer. He could not be ranked among the great inventors, and the features of Great Western locomotive practice of later days that were uniquely his own were very few. His genius lay not only in recognising a good thing when he saw it, but in the skilful application of it to his own particular problems. He was far removed from an egoist, and like many distinguished men of strong personality he was ready to listen attentively to the views of his staff, even down to the level of draughtsmen, works chargehands, drivers and firemen. By the year 1896 he had become very interested in American locomotive practice, particularly in the development of very large boilers. When this delicate task was

The first Badminton, No 3292, built December 1897, and nameless until April 1898. *(British Railways)*

assigned to him, with the definite idea that one day he would succeed Dean, he began, with the covert approbation of the Board, to make plans for the complete modernisation of the locomotive stock. At the same time, out of human considerations it was necessary to avoid giving any outward impression that the reins were gradually being taken out of Dean's hands. In beginning his great development of the Swindon boiler two features of past history favoured the impression that some of it was a logical development of Dean's earlier work, and indeed that of Daniel Gooch. A firebox raised above the level of the boiler stemmed from broad gauge days, while not only Gooch, but Dean himself had built locomotives with domeless boilers.

The hand of Churchward first became apparent in the design of the Badminton class of express passenger 4-4-0 the first of which, No 3292, was completed at Swindon in December 1897. This was originally conceived as a 6ft 8½in version of the Armstrongs, with smaller cylinders, and a boiler with high raised round-topped firebox, and the extended smokebox of the Dukes. But from his studies of American practice Churchward had become convinced of the advantages of the Belpaire type of firebox, in the greater steam space afforded above the water line, and in the simpler arrangements of staying the inside firebox, and so, at a late stage the design of the Badmintons was changed to include a Belpaire firebox. The result was a locomotive that so far as appearances went was something of a misfit. A. G. Robbins writing in *The Railway Magazine* of 1899 commented thus:

A very large Belpaire firebox hardly improves the appearance of the engine, but gives ample

The experimental 4-4-0 No 3312 *Bulldog* as originally built in October 1898. *(Locomotive Publishing Co)*

grate area. The overhung springs and extended smokebox are far from pleasing features in the design, and here they are particularly aggressive. It is a curious anomaly that a line which possesses in its 'singles' some of the handsomest engines in the world should produce coupled engines which can hardly be termed other than hideous.

Looks apart, and one can hardly agree with such severe condemnation as the foregoing, the Badmintons were splendid locomotives in traffic. Their early work is fortunately well documented, but before discussing details of individual runs, reference must be made to two further essays by Churchward in domed boilers with raised Belpaire fireboxes. These were the isolated No 3312 *Bulldog*, completed at Swindon in October 1898, and the last four of the Duke class Nos 3328-3331, built at Swindon in July-August 1899. Details of these three types of boiler were as follows:

The boiler used on the Bulldog is generally considered as the first prototype of Churchward's Standard No 2, which was followed by the first domeless variant on No 3310 *Waterford* of the Badminton class, built in January 1899.

No 3292 was evidently regarded as a prototype, and it remained the only one of the class for nearly five months. During that time also it was nameless. But when production began in earnest the next eleven, Nos 3293-3303, were turned out in three months. In July 1898 Swindon, at one per week, was almost rivalling Crewe's rate of locomotive production. The pioneer locomotive was named *Badminton* in April 1898 and gave its name to the class while the production eleven had a varied collection of names, thus:

3293	*Barrington*	3299	*Hubbard*
3294	*Blenheim*	3300	*Hotspur*
3295	*Bessborough*	3301	*Monarch*
3296	*Cambria*	3302	*Mortimer*
3297	*Earl Cawdor*	3303	*Marlborough*
3298	*Grosvenor*		

Domed Boilers: Raised Belpaire Firebox

Type	Badminton	Bulldog	Dukes 3328-3331
TUBES: Number	244	290	244
Outside diameter—in	1⅝	1⅝	1⅝
HEATING SURFACES:			
Tubes—sq in	1175.32	1395.62	1174.25
Firebox—sq in	121.58	124.41	115.60
GRATE AREA: sq ft	18.32	23.65	18.37
BOILER PRESSURE: lb/sq in	180	180	180

No 3302 *Mortimer*, in photographic grey, showing the standard form of the Badminton class. *(British Railways)*

The names were mostly connected with the directorate, Earl Cawdor then being Chairman, while Nos 3299 and 3302 had the Christian names of their owners added later, otherwise No 3302 might have been mistaken for a station name. The last eight locomotives of the class were turned out from Swindon between September 1898 and January 1899, and it was the last but one of these that had the special domeless boiler.

3304	*Oxford*	3308	*Savernake*
3305	*Samson*	3309	*Shakespeare*
3306	*Shelburne*	3310	*Waterford*
3307	*Shrewsbury*	3311	*Wynnstay*

Nos 3304 and 3307 had their names removed in the 'purge' by the Traffic Department, but *Badminton*, *Marlborough* and *Savernake*

Badminton class 4-4-0 No 3308 *Savernake* in original livery. *(L & GRP)*

escaped. Why, it is hard to explain, when as told earlier in this book remote Cornish village names were removed because it was feared they might confuse the travelling public. One might equally have said the same about the name of No 3310, when the Waterford Boat Express was one of the high prestige trains leaving Paddington. On a point of detail, they were the first Great Western locomotives to have curved nameplates carried above the splashers, except in the case of *Waterford*, which for some reason had a large combined number and nameplate carried on the cab side.

Personalia apart, the Badmintons were excellent locomotives in traffic. They were allocated to the fast express routes having gradients that the single-wheelers found trying, such as the London-Wolverhampton trains that ran via Worcester, and the West-to-North route via the Severn Tunnel. Their machinery was apparently the same as that of the Armstrongs with the inside and outside cranks in line, and the same arrangement of the slide valves beneath the cylinders. But there was a 'something' in them that made them just as fast

Birmingham express (via Oxford) on Goring troughs hauled by No 3297 *Earl Cawdor,* in original condition. *(L & GRP)*

s the Armstrongs were sluggish. They had ample port openings, and a direct exhaust from the valves between the cylinders and upwards straight to the blastpipe, and they used to attain speeds well in excess of 80mph. A. G. Robbins made a number of footplate journeys on Great Western locomotives just at the end of the nineteenth century, and logged a couple of very fast runs on the so-called 'Wool-buyers' Special' which used to be run from Bradford to Bristol, for the wool merchants of the north to attend wool sales in that city. The Great Western and the North Western in partnership used to run a highly competitive train against the Midland, which of course had the advantage of a direct run up their own main line throughout. The LNWR and GWR joint train was not a heavy one, but with Badminton class engines it was run between Shrewsbury and Bristol at speeds that have not been known since over that difficult route. Mr Robbins rode on No 3301 *Monarch* on the outward and home trips on the special in 1899, when the southbound train was booked to leave Shrewsbury at 2.50pm, arriving at Bristol 5.17pm. On the following day the return train left at 4.30pm and was due at Shrewsbury at 6.55pm. In each direction the train consisted of five coaches: two brake-thirds, a composite, and two dining cars, totalling 126.7 tons tare.

The accompanying table sets out details of the outbound run from Shrewsbury to Hereford. The long and severe ascent to Church Stretton is anything but favourable to an engine starting 'cold' on a long and fast run, and despite the provision of the very large steam dome, *Monarch* was priming at the start. The first two miles took nearly five minutes and it was not until the train was up the initial 1 in 127 gradient that this powerful locomotive really got to grips with its relatively light load. But on the easier pitch between Condover and Dorrington speed rose to 55mph and the 1 in 90 that follows would have been cleared at over 40mph but for a relaying slack above Leebotwood. Then from

GWR: SHREWSBURY-HEREFORD
Wool Buyers' Special
No 3301 *Monarch*
Load: 135 tons gross

Distance Miles		Actual min sec		Speeds mph
0.0	SHREWSBURY	0	00	—
4.2	Condover	8	39	35
6.4	Dorrington	11	16	54
9.3	Leebotwood	15	08	40 1/2
		pws		—
12.8	Church Stretton	20	37	35
19.9	CRAVEN ARMS	27	15	78/72
22.9	Onibury	29	30	77
27.5	Ludlow	33	29	60*
32.1	Woofferton	37	31	72/61
38.4	LEOMINSTER	43	17	69/65
44.0	*Milepost 44*	48	36	60
46.8	Moreton-on-Lugg	51	07	68
50.0	*Milepost 50*	54	13	60
51.0	HEREFORD	55	47	—

*Speed restriction

No 3296 *Cambria* at Exeter. *(L & GRP)*

Church Stretton there was a fast and undelayed downhill run to the very outskirts of Hereford, with a maximum of 78mph at Craven Arms and 77mph near Onibury. The average speed over the thirty-three miles between Mileposts 16 and 49 was 68mph and the 50.9 miles from Shrewsbury to Hereford were completed in 55 minutes 47 seconds start-to-stop. Reading a little between the lines of the contemporary account, one gathers that the riding of the

engine was distinctly lively at times, and one naturally curious to know how the Stroudle system of balancing contributed to th smoothness or otherwise of the riding at thes high speeds. There was less opportunity for fa running south of Hereford, and with so relative light a load short work was made of gradien like that from Pontrilas up to Llanvihang summit. Despite four slacks for relaying the 68. miles from Hereford to Bristol, Temple Mead were covered in 83 minutes 5 seconds to make a arrival just one minute early.

On the return journey, details of which are s out in two separate tables, interest was centre first on the climbing of the steep gradients, i stormy weather on a rough autumnal evening On the Filton bank, at 1 in 75, before the engin

GWR : BRISTOL-HEREFORD
Wool Buyers' Special
No 3301 *Monarch*
Load: 135 tons gross

Distance Miles		Actual min sec	Average Speeds mph
0.0	BRISTOL (Temple Meads)	0 00	—
2.0	Milepost 2	4 10	—
4.0	Milepost 4	7 30	33 1/2
10.0	Milepost 10	13 40	70
—		pws	30
—		pws	10
16.5	SEVERN TUNNEL JUNC	23 20	—
25.7	Maindee West Junc	33 20	67 max
—		slack	25
30.2	Milepost 37	39 05	60
34.2	Milepost 33	44 40	38
34.8	PONTYPOOL ROAD	45 40	—
—		pws	5
41.8	Penpergwm	52 45	75
44.5	Abergavenny	55 20	57
48.5	Llanvihangel	60 45	41
56.0	Pontrilas	67 10	82 max
59.2	Milepost 8	70 04	67
62.2	Milepost 5	72 42	67
65.1	Red Hill Junc	75 15	70/35*
68.4	HEREFORD	78 55	—

*Speed restriction

GWR: HEREFORD-SHREWSBURY
Wool Buyers' Special
No 3301 *Monarch*
Load: 135 tons gross

Distance Miles		Actual min sec	Averag Speeds mph
0.0	HEREFORD	0 00	—
1.0	Milepost 50	2 12	—
7.5	Dinmore	9 30	45.2
—		pws	—
10.2	Ford Bridge	12 45	49.8
12.6	LEOMINSTER	16 25	39.3
15.7	Berrington	20 05	50.7
18.9	Woofferton	23 03	64.8
22.0	Milepost 29	25 40	71.3
23.5	Ludlow	27 20	54.2
28.1	Onibury	31 40	63.7
31.1	CRAVEN ARMS	34 40	60.0
35.6	Marsh Brook	39 35	55.0
38.2	Church Stretton	42 47	48.8
41.7	Leebotwood	45 55	67.0
44.6	Dorrington	48 20	72.0
46.7	Condover	50 05	72.0
51.0	SHREWSBURY	55 45	—

No 3302 at Paddington, carrying the original shortened form of the name *Mortimer*. (*J. N. Maskelyne*)

d fully warmed up to its work, the minimum peed was 33mph, while between the Maindee nctions and Pontypool Road the slowest mile as run at 38½mph. It was after recovering om the 5mph relaying slack through Pontypool oad station that the most spectacular and xciting work of the whole round trip was erformed. In the course of many years of avelling over this route I have never seen nything remotely to approach an average speed f just over 60mph between Mileposts 31 and 11, ncluding the heavy ascent from the river rossing at Penpergwm, through Abergavenny Llanvihangel, all made in torrents of rain. peed was 75mph round the curve at enpergwm, and then fell away to a sustained 1mph on the 1 in 94 gradient above bergavenny. Then the driver fairly let the ngine go down to Pontrilas, and Robbins ocked six alternate quarter miles at 73, 80½, 2, 80½, 80½ and 75mph. He wrote: 'Owing to e darkness and driving rain I found it npossible to take any mileposts between 16 and 1; indeed I had all my work cut out to keep board the engine'. As the log shows the 33.7 iles from passing Pontypool Road at dead slow peed to arrival in Hereford took no more than 3¼ minutes and the total time from Bristol was o more than 78 minutes 55 seconds despite the

hindrances on the early stages of the run. Scheduled time was eighty-five minutes. A fine concluding run was made from Hereford to Shrewsbury, as the separate tabulation shows. Here it was the uphill work that claims most attention, particularly the time of 11 minutes 7 seconds for the 10.1 miles, steeply adverse from Onibury up to Church Stretton with its concluding average of 50mph up the final pitch from Marsh Brook, where the gradient is continuously 1 in 112. As it was, the train was brought into Shrewsbury 3½ minutes early.

While nothing approaching this standard of running was required in ordinary service from the Badminton class, it is evident from the foregoing that the design was a success, even though this was admittedly an exceptional assignment.

On the 10.45am South Wales express, of which as detailed in Chapter One *Charles*

No 3297 *Earl Cawdor*, decorated and equipped for working the Royal Train non-stop from Windsor to Dover, on 11 March 1899. The tender is provided with extra water tank capacity for making the long run. (*British Railways*)

GWR: 12.05pm EXETER-PADDINGTON
No 3298 *Grosvenor*
Load 165 tons

Distance Miles		Actual min sec	Average speeds mph
0.0	EXETER	0 00	—
3.5	Stoke Canon	6 17	—
7.2	Silverton	10 27	53.2
8.4	Hele	11 53	50.3
12.6	Cullompton	16 15	57.4
14.8	Tiverton Junc	18 59	49.1
19.9	*Whiteball Box*	25 26	47.3
23.7	Wellington	29 16	59.5
28.8	Norton Fitzwarren	33 04	80.5
30.8	TAUNTON	34 48	69.1*
36.6	Durston	41 16	53.3
42.3	Bridgwater	46 40	63.4
44.9	Dunball	49 10	62.4
—		pws	—
48.6	Highbridge	55 12	37.0
55.3	Bleadon	62 06	58.3
58.8	*Worle Junc*	65 18	65.7
63.6	Yatton	69 56	62.1
67.5	Nailsea	73 44	61.6
69.9	Flax Bourton	75 57	64.9
74.5	Bedminster	80 26	62.1
75.2	*Pylle Hill Junc*	81 56	27.9*
77.9	*Bristol East*	86 26	36.0
80.1	Keynsham	89 59	37.1
82.5	Saltford	92 45	52.2
87.0	BATH	97 23	57.8*
89.3	Bathampton	100 48	40.2
92.0	Box	103 56	51.8
95.6	Corsham	108 46	46.4
99.9	Chippenham	113 52	38.8
106.2	Dauntsey	119 24	68.4
111.0	Wootton Bassett	124 56	52.0
116.4	SWINDON	130 59	53.5
122.1	Shrivenham	136 32	61.6
127.2	Uffington	141 00	68.3
129.8	Challow	143 18	67.8
133.3	Wantage Road	146 12	72.3
137.2	Steventon	149 29	71.6
140.6	DIDCOT	152 16	73.2
—		slack	—
152.2	Pangbourne	165 22	53.1
157.7	READING	171 17	55.9
—		slack	—
169.5	Maidenhead	185 47	49.0
175.2	Slough	191 09	63.8
184.6	Southall	200 13	62.2
188.0	Ealing Broadway	203 24	62.2
193.7	PADDINGTON	209 56	

* Speed restrictions, at Taunton, on Bristol avoiding line, and through Bath.

Saunders made such heavy weather, *Badminton* itself just romped away with a load of 178 tons, reaching Bath in 118¼ minutes despite two permanent way checks, while on the corresponding up train, *Barrington* with 204 tons, leaving Bath ten minutes late, and running against a side gale with sleet and snow reached Paddington 5¾ minutes early—119 minutes 20 seconds from Bath. Rous-Marten went down to

One of the 3521 class 5ft 2in 4-4-0s, No 3537, fitted with boiler with flush-top Belpaire firebox. *(W. J. Reynolds)*

Exeter to log the 12.05pm up non-stop to Paddington. There seems no doubt that a special show was put on for his benefit, for the train arrived in Paddington just 15 minutes early, and could have been much more had not the driver eased down very much after passing Didcot. A detailed log is shown above, not as an example of everyday running, but to indicate what these fine engines could do. A maximum of 83½mph was attained down the Wellington bank, and a good steady speed on the level between Taunton and Bristol. There was also

No 3310 *Waterford,* as originally built, with domeless boiler and high raised Belpaire firebox. *(British Railways)*

some particularly free running between Didcot and Swindon. Rous-Marten estimated that another eight minutes could have been cut from the schedule if the effort had been sustained eastwards from Didcot; but a possible arrival in Paddington twenty-three minutes early was a little too much to expect!

While these new locomotives were getting into their stride in 1899, there was produced at Swindon one of the most extraordinary classes of 4-4-0 ever to run in Great Britain—extraordinary that is in their genealogy, rather than in their technical details. But when a broad gauge 'convertible' 0-4-2 tank first gets itself changed into a 0-4-4, is then converted to standard gauge, and finally turned back to front to become a 4-4-0 tender engine it would seem that all the possibilities of rebuilding have been exhausted. Here, of course, I am concerned only with the end product, or rather the beginning of the life of the 3521 class, as 4-4-0s. There were

forty engines in the numerical series 3521 to 3560, but not all were at first treated in the same way. Twenty-six were fitted with the type of domed boiler then standard on the Dean goods 2301 class, with flush round-topped firebox, and a moderate sized dome at the forward end. They retained the original 5ft 2in coupled wheels, though there can have been little else of the original tank engines left. They had the standard 17in by 24in cylinders used on so many of the smaller Dean classes, and the slide valves working on vertical faces between the cylinders were actuated by direct Stephenson link motion.

Waterford in original condition, save for removal of safety-valve lever, on an up express at Bath. *(L & GRP)*

The bogies were of the same general type as developed for the 4-2-2 and 4-4-0 express engines, but having wheels of the small diameter of 2ft 8in, as compared to 3ft 8in on the Dukes and 4ft 1in on the Armstrongs. The new engines, for new they were in everything except name, were at first sent down to the West of England to take up the work on light and branch line duties on which their 0-4-4 tank predecessors had gained an unenviable reputation for derailment. Others worked in the Bristol Division.

Before referring to the rebuilding to which the remaining fourteen of the original engines were subjected, it is time to turn to Churchward's programme of boiler development, which began with the construction of *Bulldog* in October 1898. His hand was shown a little more clearly with the Badminton class No 3310 *Waterford*, built in January 1899, which had the high raised Belpaire firebox, as on the other Badmintons and *Bulldog*, but with a domeless parallel boiler, and the safety-valve at the rearward end of the barrel. This was a departure for the Great Western, because on the many engines previously built with domeless boilers, both broad and standard gauge, the safety-valves had been over the firebox, and the boiler barrels themselves 'straightbacks'. Churchward was

First of the domeless boilered 5ft 8in 4-4-0s, No 3352 *Camel*: note additional number plate on smokebox. *(W. Beckerlegge)*

clearly feeling his way with *Waterford*. The provision of a steam dome—particularly of the size standard on the most recent Great Western locomotives—introduced a point of weakness in the construction of the boiler, and since he was already looking ahead to boilers carrying considerably higher pressures than customary hitherto at Swindon there was every reason to avoid any points of weakness, if possible. Those who argued against the use of domeless boilers, and criticised, among others, those of Patrick Stirling on the Great Northern Railway, frequently pointed to the liability to priming as a disadvantage; but as the footplate observations on *Monarch* showed, even the presence of a huge dome did not prevent an expert driver from experiencing some priming at the start of a run.

The varying boiler dimensions of Churchward's first locomotives show the extent to which experimenting was in progress. I have previously quoted the dimensions of *Bulldog*'s original boiler, but at one time the heating surface was considerably larger, by the use of 286 tubes of $1\frac{7}{8}$in diameter, giving a tube heating surface of 1589.5sq ft. But this arrangement was evidently found to be too crowded, and to give nominal heating surface at the expense of a reduced volume for circulation of the water; the later arrangement, with 290 tubes of $1\frac{5}{8}$in diameter, was the same as on the *Waterford*, even though the latter had the domeless barrel. *Waterford*'s boiler proved no more than the penultimate

One of the 5ft 2in 4-4-0s of the 3521 class, with Camel type boiler. *(British Railways)*

stage in the development of the parallel version of the Swindon Standard No 2, which appeared in its final form on No 3352 *Camel* in October 1899. The barrel was the same size as that of *Waterford*, but had 277 tubes of 1⅞in diameter and the total heating surfaces were, tubes 1538.06sq ft, firebox 124.96sq ft, while the grate area was reduced to 21.45sq ft against 23.65sq ft. *Camel* (which was named after the river, and had nothing to do with war in the desert) was followed between November 1899 and March 1900 by twenty more, Nos 3332-3351, but detailed reference to this large and important class as it ultimately became is deferred to the next chapter. At this stage, however, I may add that the remaining fourteen conversions of the 3521 class, of 5ft 2in 4-4-0s, were rebuilt from tank engines and fitted with Camel type parallel domeless boilers in 1900-2.

CHAPTER FOUR

CAMELS : ATBARAS

Camel, and the twenty locomotives that followed, Nos 3332-51, could quite correctly have been described as Dukes with domeless boilers. They had the same shape of outside framing, handsomely curved over the coupled wheel axleboxes, and had the same bogies, cylinders and motion. The wheelbase was the same. The boilers had the circular drumhead type of smokebox, supported on the curved-sided saddle that became such a characteristic feature of Great Western inside-cylinder 4-4-0s. There was still indecision as to how to display the names, and all the twenty-one Camels with curved outside frames had oval combined number and nameplates on the cab sides, making the names a little difficult to recognise when running past at full speed. *Camel* itself had additional number plates on the centre line of the smokebox. The twenty succeeding locomotives of this first batch carried the following names:

4-4-0 No 3338 *Laira,* showing the standard form of the first batch of Camels. *(British Railways)*

3332	*Avalon*	3342	*Orion*
3333	*Brasenose*	3343	*Pegasus*
3334	*Eclipse*	3344	*Pluto*
3335	*Etona*	3345	*Perseus*
3336	*Glastonbury*	3346	*Tavy*
3337	*Kenilworth*	3347	*Tregothnan*
3338	*Laira*	3348	*Titan*
3339	*Marco Polo*	3349	*The Wolf*
3340	*Marazion*	3350	*Swift*
3341	*Mars*	3351	*Sedgemoor*

Nos 3336, 3337, 3338, and 3347 lost their names in one or another of the Traffic Department 'purges'. Presumably *Laira* was considered a snare to guileless enginemen, tempted to hitch a lift back to their home shed: how stupid can officialdom get!

After the completion of No 3351 *Sedgemoor* in March 1900, there was a pause of two months in the building of 5ft 8in 4-4-0s, during which the first of a new class of 6ft 8in engines appeared, No 3373 *Atbara*. With these locomotives the flowing curves of Great Western express types, which had begun to disappear with the Badmintons, went for ever, because the Atbaras had a straight-topped running plate that extended unbrokenly from the footplate to a point level with the rearward bogie wheel. Furthermore, when construction of the Camels continued in May 1900, it was seen that they too had the straight-topped frames. Production of the two classes continued almost simultaneously during the rest of the year 1900, as follows:

Rear end view of *Laira* in photographic grey, showing lining on tender. *(British Railways)*

Month	Atbaras	Camels
April	4	—
May	6	1
June	—	4
July	3	—
August	5	—
September	2	—
October	—	4
November	—	8
December	—	3

After that 'drive', in which forty new passenger locomotives had been turned out in nine months, there was a pause before the second large batch of Atbaras began to issue from Swindon. But while the new 6ft 8in engines, and

No 3373 *Atbara* as originally built, at Westbourne Park sheds. *(British Railways)*

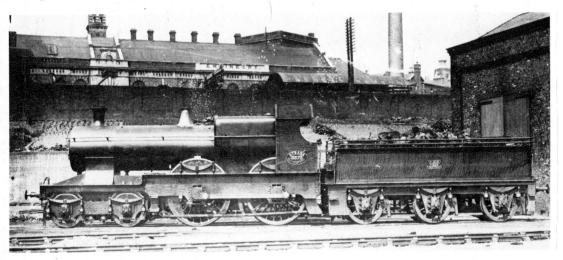

Up West of England express on the single-line section between Teignmouth and Dawlish: locomotive No 3332 *Avalon*. (L & GRP)

the 5ft 8in type from No 3353 onwards looked very much alike, and had the same boiler, the Atbaras had the same crank arrangement as the Badmintons whereas the Camels had that of the Dukes. The arrangement of the machinery and framing of the Atbaras may be studied from the drawings on pages 46 and 47, while a very complete set of dimensional details is given on page 94. I wonder what Churchward thought of the following comment, in one of the most authoritative technical journals of the day: 'The boilers are of the Belpaire type, and so far as height and width are concerned, are of the maximum dimensions possible with the present loading gauge'. Generally, however, very little notice was taken of the introduction of the domeless-boilered 4-4-0s on the GWR. The

technical press of the day was so taken up with the latest Webb compounds from Crewe, Dunalastairs from St Rollox, and the Worsdell engines from Gateshead, and there was a very genuine feeling that the newest Great Western products were unnecessarily ugly.

One can be a little curious as to why Churchward retained double frames, when he was clearly so partial to American practice in other respects. Although by the year 1900 he was becoming more and more in charge of affairs at Swindon, one feels that the general introduction of domeless boilers was enough in the way of major change while Dean was still there. His major development was centred on the boiler, and the double-frame arrangement was well tried, familiar to the shops and needed little or no drawing office work for the new locomotives. The plan view of the Atbara frame shows clearly the centre support for the bogie, and how little interference it afforded to access to the slide valves once the bogie itself had been run clear. The actual valve dimensions were standard on all the inside-cylinder 4-4-0s while they retained

An *Atbara* in photographic grey: No 3375 *Edgcumbe*. (British Railways)

slide valves. Both Camels and Atbaras had much wider cabs than the Dukes and Badmintons, so much so that the overhung springs of the rear coupled wheels passed inside the cab. By comparison with older Great Western engines the cabs were quite roomy though the shelter they provided was scant. As originally built they had steam-operated reversing gear. The nominal tractive effort, with 180 lb/sq in boiler pressure was no greater than that of the Badmintons, and considering the moderate loads of the principal express trains, which will be more apparent when I come to some actual details of their running, their coal consumption was not particularly light. In 1901 it was reported that the average consumption of those in the link at the Paddington old shed was 32.6 lb per train mile.

The naming of the twenty Atbaras built at Swindon in 1900 followed popular sentiment of the day, and included names that were then on everyone's lips. But like many of the Crewe names bestowed in comparable circumstances the significance of a number of them faded with the years; while few would continue to have doubts about *Baden Powell, Kitchener* or *Roberts, Powerful* and *Terrible* might conjure up thoughts far removed from the armoured cruisers that played a part in the South African campaign. It is interesting to see that names chosen from both the Sudanese and South African wars were grouped together and applied more or less alphabetically, with one or two 'outsiders', as it were, interspersed.

3373	*Atbara*	3383	*Kekewich*
3374	*Baden Powell*	3384	*Omdurman*
3375	*Conqueror*	3385	*Powerful*
3376	*Herschell*	3386	*Pembroke*
3377	*Kitchener*	3387	*Roberts*
3378	*Khartoum*	3388	*Sir Redvers*
3379	*Kimberley*	3389	*Sir Daniel*
3380	*Ladysmith*	3390	*Terrible*
3381	*Maine*	3391	*Wolseley*
3382	*Mafeking*	3392	*White*

The Atbaras differed from the Badmintons only in their boilers, and it was not surprising that they proved equally fast runners. Rous-Marten made a number of trips specially to see what could be got out of them, and claimed on one occasion a maximum of 97mph. On another, Driver David Hughes, who had such a distinguished record of achievement with the 2-2-2 No 162 *Cobham*, put on a special show with the pioneer No 3373 *Atbara* on the morning Paddington-Birmingham non-stop, which was then allowed 143 minutes for the 129.3 miles, via Oxford. With a load of 180 tons the train passed

A name that could be misconstrued! Atbara No 3390 *Terrible* in original condition. (L & GRP)

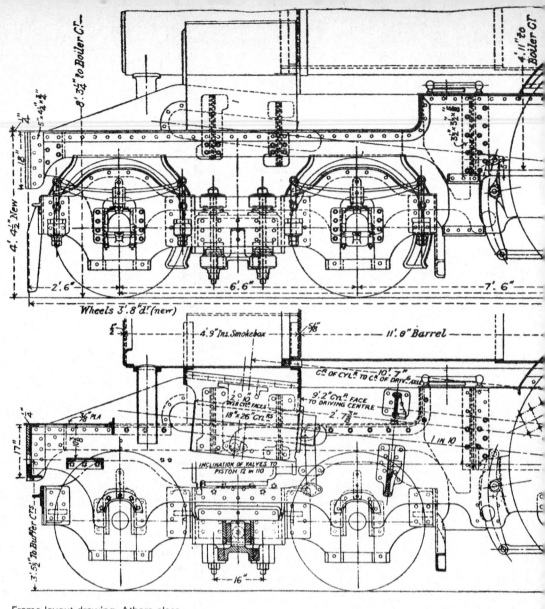

Frame layout drawing, Atbara class.

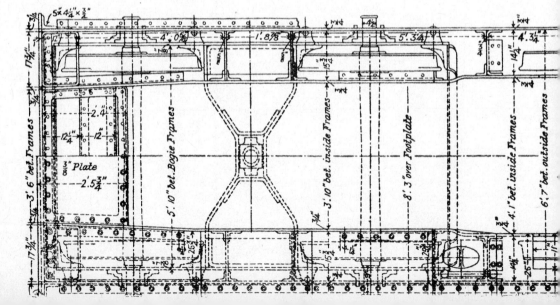

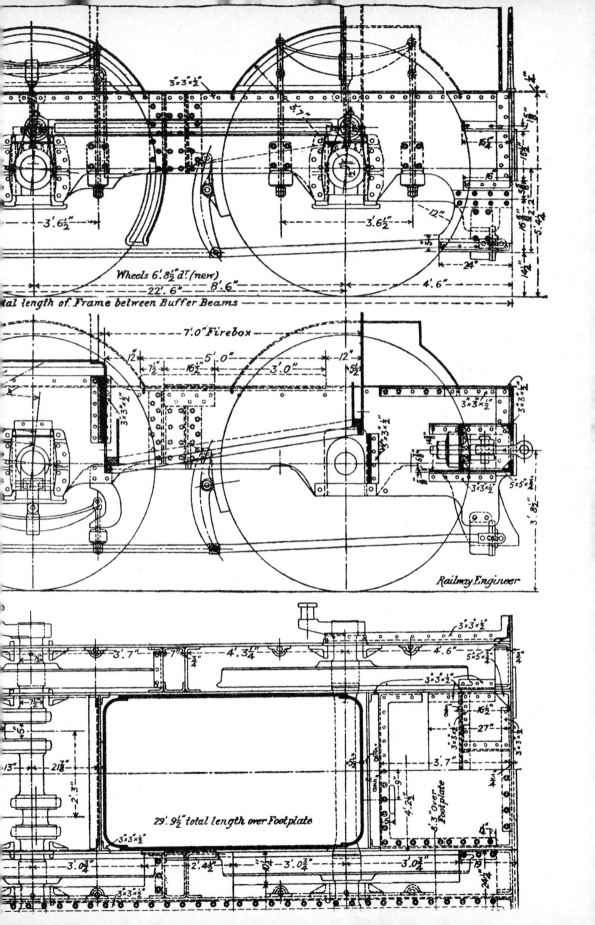

Wheels 6'.8½" d." (new)

22'.6"   8'.6"

Total length of Frame between Buffer Beams

7'.0" Firebox

5'.0"

3'.0"

Railway Engineer

3'.7"   4'.3¼"   4'.6"

29'. 9½" total length over Footplate

Leamington, 106 miles, in 107 minutes 35 seconds despite four signal checks and a dead stand lasting for three minutes in Radley station. Although he was getting far ahead of time the driver continued to press on vigorously, only to experience more signal checks, and finally a dead stand lasting for 6½ minutes at Bordesley. The train eventually drew into Snow Hill in 141½ minutes from Paddington. The net time was 119½ minutes, representing an average of 65mph. On the strength of this there was much talk of a two-hour schedule, via Oxford, which Driver Hughes more than once expressed himself quite ready to do, with an Atbara.

More normal runs with the new engines gave net average speeds of 56 to 58mph and the following table gives details of four runs of very fine quality on the Bristol and West of England service, all made in 1901, before the introduction of the Cornish Riviera Express.

The outstanding event of 1902, and undoubtedly the pinnacle of fame achieved by the Atbara class locomotives, was of course the Royal visit to Devonshire in March, in the course of which the longest non-stop runs yet attempted on the Great Western Railway were successfully made. The down train, on 7 March, was run non-stop over the 228.5 miles from Paddington to Kingswear, while on the return, on 10 March, the special was worked non-stop over the 246.4 miles from Millbay Crossing to Paddington. The five coaches of the train had a tare weight of 127 tons, and were worked on both the long non-stop runs by No 3374, specially renamed Britannia for the occasion, with Driver Burden in charge. Scheduled time for the down journey was 285 minutes, but with King Edward taking great personal interest in the running of the train, and having no inhibitions about speed the train was allowed to run somewhat ahead of time, and

RUNS WITH *ATBARA* CLASS LOCOMOTIVES — 1901

Route	No	Locomotive Name	Load tons	Distance miles	Actual min	sec	Net time min	Net Average Speed mph
Paddington-Exeter*	3392	White	150	193.6	211	44	204	57.0
Exeter-Paddington*	3380	Ladysmith	240	193.6	209	14	201	57.8
Bristol-Exeter	3377	Kitchener	240	75.5	80	41	80 3/4	56.1
Bristol-Paddington†	3409	Quebec	180	118.4	128	56	123	57.6

* via Bristol avoiding line   † via Bath

No 3374, normally *Baden Powell*, but renamed *Britannia* and decorated for the Royal Train of 1902. (British Railways)

GWR ROYAL TRAIN : 7 March 1902
No 3374 *Britannia*
Load: — 127 tons tare

Distance Miles		Actual min	Average Speed mph
0.0	Paddington	0	—
31.0	Twyford	34	54.8
36.2	*Reading West Junc*	39	62.5
53.1	Didcot	56	59.7
77.3	Swindon	80	60.6
106.9	Bath	110 1/2	58.2
118.4	*Pylle Hill Junc*	127	41.8
137.75	*Uphill Junc*	146	55.2
162.85	Taunton	171 1/2	59.1
193.6	Exeter	206 1/2	52.9
213.8	Newton Abbot	234 1/2	43.3
228.5	Kingswear	262 1/2	31.5

reached Kingswear more than 20 minutes early. It will be seen that a notably steady average of around 60mph was maintained on the open stretches of line, and that the average from Paddington to Exeter of 56mph was much the same as that of service runs made with the down *Cornishman*, as shown by the run of *White* in the table on page 48. The Royal party continued to Plymouth the same day. No 3374 worked the train back to Newton Abbot and from there, after reversal of direction, the engine was a *Camel*, No 3357 *Exeter*, renamed *Royal Sovereign* specially for the occasion.

On Monday, 10 March the return journey to London was made, and the times run are shown in a further log. Again very steady speed was maintained throughout, and the average of 52.2mph from Millbay to Paddington was an excellent effort in train operation, although not involving any exceptional locomotive work. In assessment of the performance it must be recalled that at that time severe speed restrictions were called for through Exeter and

GWR ROYAL TRAIN
10 March 1902
No 3374 *Britannia*
Load: — 127 tons tare

Distance Miles		Actual min	Average Speed mph
0.0	Millbay Crossing	0	—
32.6	Newton Abbot	47	41.5
52.8	Exeter	75	43.3
83.55	Taunton	109 1/2	53.5
108.65	*Uphill Junc*	137	54.8
129.45	*Bristol East Depot*	159 1/2	55.5
139.5	Bath	172	48.4
169.1	Swindon	203	57.1
193.4	Didcot East	227	61.0
210.2	*Reading West Junc*	245 1/2	55.5
215.4	Twyford	251	56.8
246.4	Paddington	284	56.3

Taunton stations, in addition to the slacks for single-line token exchange on the South Devon line between Dawlish and Teignmouth. Furthermore, at His Majesty's request, the train slowed down passing Swindon Works so that he could see better, and acknowledge the acclaim of the vast numbers of railwaymen who had been allowed briefly to leave their duties in the works and see the royal train go by. By way of anticipation I may add that when the Cornish Riviera Express was put on in 1904 the timing from Plymouth North Road, to Paddington was 265 minutes, with a running time of 195 minutes for the 193.6 miles up from Exeter.

Although the new City class engines were then available, the Atbaras took their turn on this celebrated train, and with the moderate loads first conveyed the running of the two classes of 4-4-0 was indistinguishable. I have tabulated the journal times of three down journeys made

GWR CORNISH RIVIERA EXPRESS
ATBARA CLASS LOCOMOTIVES
Load: 6 coaches, 146 tons tare

Locomotive No Locomotive Name			3386 Pembroke	3380 Ladysmith	3407 Malta
Distance Miles		Schedule min	Actual min	Actual min	Actual min
0.0	Paddington	0	0	0	0
18.5	Slough	20 1/2	20	20	21
—			—	—	sigs
36.0	Reading	36	36	37	42
53.1	Didcot	53	51	53	58
77.3	Swindon	77	75	76	82
106.9	Bath	106	104	102	109
118.7	Pylle Hill Junc	120	118	117	123
137.7	Uphill Junc	139	137	134	142
162.8	Taunton	163	161	158	165
193.6	Exeter	197	194	192	196
213.7	Newton Abbot	222 1/2	220	220	221
245.6	Plymouth	267	264	266	265

during the first month the train ran. On the first of these it will be seen that *Pembroke* drew gradually ahead of time after Reading, and ran between two and three minutes early all the way to Plymouth, without any exceptional running. *Ladysmith* ran fast in the early stages, passing Bath four minutes early, but easing down thereafter, while in the last column *Malta* was badly checked by adverse signals between Slough and Reading, and passed the latter station six minutes late. After that, however, the lateness was reduced to five minutes at Swindon, three at Bath, two at Taunton, and one minute early by Exeter, through an obviously very fine effort from Taunton, and a time of only thirty-one minutes for the 30.8 miles, including the climb from Norton Fitzwarren to Whiteball box. On this run the average speed over the 157.6

Up West of England express slowing down to enter the single line section at Parsons Rock Tunnel: No 3371 *Tregeagle. (R. Brookman)*

miles from Reading to Exeter was 61.3mph, while the net time of 259 minutes throughout from Paddington to Plymouth is equal to 57mph.

On the up road *Malta* was one of the engines working the train during its first week, when the crew had the misfortune to sustain damage to the water pick-up scoop at Starcross troughs after having made a fast start and passed Taunton five minutes early. A stop was made at Swindon to take water, but apparently there was more trouble, for a second stop was made at Reading, for a fresh engine, and the journey was completed with a 7ft 8in single No 3069 *Earl of Chester*—probably the only occasion on which

the Cornish Riviera Express was ever worked by a single-wheeler. As an example of normal working in the early days of the train, I have tabulated the running of *Pembroke*, on which good speed was made throughout and an arrival 2½ minutes early effected. It will be seen that a minute was dropped on the sharp allowance of thirty-one minutes from Exeter to Taunton, but with a fine spurt from Swindon to Didcot the train was four minutes early at the latter place. The average speed over this 24.2 miles was 69.2mph.

The workings of the train in Cornwall are of interest as showing what was required of the Camel class locomotives. Here again the older variety with parallel domeless boilers was used turn and turn about the later type having Churchward's first form of the tapered boiler. The timings were then as follows:

GWR CORNISH RIVIERA EXPRESS
No 3386 *Pembroke*
Load: 146 tons tare

Distance Miles		Schedule min	Actual min
0.0	Plymouth	0	0
31.9	Newton Abbot	44 1/2	43 1/2
52.0	Exeter	70	67
82.8	Taunton	101	99
107.9	Uphill Junc	124	122
126.9	Pylle Hill Junc	143	142
138.7	Bath	158	156
168.3	Swindon	189	187
192.5	Didcot	212	208
209.6	Reading	229	225
227.1	Slough	245	242 1/2
245.6	Paddington	265	262 1/2

Distance Miles		Time Down min	Time Up min
0.0	Plymouth	0	90
34.7	Par	58	30
53.7	Truro	89	27
15.2	Gwinear Road	27	11
5.0	St. Erth	8	10
5.6	Penzance	11	0

Apropos of engine names being mistaken for train destinations, the engines working the train westward from Plymouth during the first week were, successively, *Paddington, Taunton, Marazion, Birkenhead, Albany* and *Reading*. On the up journey, and more appropriately,

River Fal and River Plym were regular locomotives. The time allowance between Plymouth and Truro was more generous than it afterwards became, but at the western end of the line the bookings remained much the same throughout steam days. The load limit for one 4-4-0 engine west of Newton Abbot was eight bogie coaches, which in practice meant about 220 tons gross. With the heavy summer holiday trains a good deal of double heading was necessary, usually with a Duke piloting a Camel.

Although much of the more spectacular work of the Atbaras was done with relatively light

A Camel of 1903, No 3419, with the new style of nameplate, before the name was added. *(L & GRP)*

loads, there did not seem to be any severe restrictions on loading between Paddington and Exeter. Generally speaking it was only on the non-stop trains to Exeter and beyond that one locomotive worked through from Paddington to the West. On all other trains, locomotives were changed at Bristol. It sometimes happened that

Camel No 3416 *Bibby,* Later renamed *Frank Bibby.* *(P. J. T. Reed)*

The Camel boiler applied to a Badminton: No 3293
Barrington, as running 1904 to 1910. *(L & GRP)*

a heavy train had been brought down from
London by one of Churchward's experimental
4-6-0s and had to be taken forward from Bristol
by a 4-4-0. This happened one day when Rous-
Marten was travelling by the 10.50am from
Paddington, and an Atbara, No 3388 *Sir
Redvers,* had a load of 350 tons to take on to
Exeter. Schedule time for the run of 75.6 miles
was then eighty-five minutes, involving an
average speed of 53.4mph, but the question was
whether the driver would attempt to take such a
load up the Wellington bank without assistance.
A splendid start was made out of Bristol, with a
speed of 45mph up the Flax Bourton bank. A
maximum of 72mph down the ensuing descent
took the train through Yatton (twelve miles) in
16 minutes 35 seconds, and fine speed followed
over the level to Taunton. Here the 32.8 miles
were covered in 31 minutes 11 seconds with

No 3419 with the ultimate standard type of nameplate:
Evan Llewellyn. (British Railways)

speed ranging between 60 and 65mph and the
44.8 miles from Bristol start occupied 47 minutes
46 seconds. For an engine of such modest
proportions, hauling 350 tons, this was really
excellent work.

If assistance was to be taken up to Whiteball a
stop would have been made at Taunton, but the
train went through at full speed, and on the
gradually steepening approach gradients had
not fallen below 47mph by Wellington station.
Then came the crucial test, and on the critical
length to the northern end of Whiteball Tunnel
speed fell to 21mph which speed was sustained
on the 1 in 127 gradient through the tunnel itself
to the signal box at the summit. The time of
16 minutes 15 seconds for the 10.9 miles up from
Taunton was excellent in such conditions of
loading, and according to Rous-Marten there
was no slipping, or any hesitancy about the way
in which the engine kept its feet on that steep
gradient of 1 in 80, leading to the tunnel.
Admittedly the weather was good. On a wet or
stormy day it is doubtful if the driver would have
attempted it. The run was concluded by a fast
descent to Exeter, covering the 19.9 miles in

exactly 18 minutes pass to stop, to complete the run from Bristol in 82 minutes 1 second, or three minutes less than schedule time.

Although the running of the Ocean Mails in 1904 is dealt with in some detail in respect of the City class, mention may be made of one fast run in which an Atbara was involved. This took place on 18 April 1904, at a time when the trains were stopping in Temple Meads station, Bristol, to change locomotives there. On that occasion No 3396 *Brisbane* took over, and with three vans, about 90 tons, ran the 118.4 miles to Paddington non-stop in 109 minutes. The successive average speeds from Swindon, as

special trains, and had its name changed appropriately. When the City Imperial Volunteers (CIVs) made their triumphant return from the war on 29 October 1900 four trains were run from Southampton, worked by the LSWR to Basingstoke, and thence to Paddington. Atbara class engines were used for all four specials, and the names selected were *Pretoria*, *Roberts*, *Powerful* and *Maine*, taking the four trains in that order. Of the four, however, only *Roberts* had its true number. *Pretoria* was named specially, and was originally No 3389; *Powerful* was transferred temporarily from No 3385, and *Maine* was put on to *Atbara* itself. But

Atbara No 3375 *Edgcumbe* with the intermediate style of nameplate. (*O. S. Nock collection*)

given by the times from the guard's journal, were 72.5mph to Didcot, 60mph on to Reading—suggesting a check of some kind on that section—and 67.8mph from Reading to the top at Paddington. The mails were generally making times of between thirteen and fourteen minutes between Didcot and Reading at that time, representing average speeds of between 73 and 78mph. If indeed *Brisbane* was checked, a net time of about 106 minutes could be claimed from Temple Meads to Paddington—67mph average speed.

No 3374 seems to have been a favourite for

as they all then had the combined oval name and number plate on the cab sides there were no clues for lineside spotters to pick up, as in the case of the famous substitution of *Windsor Castle* by *Bristol Castle* on the Royal funeral train of 1952. It was different with the three subsequent and temporary re-namings of

Camel No 3415 with the original name, *Baldwin*, later *Alfred Baldwin*, at Newton Abbot, in front of the site of the publisher's premises. (*W. Beckerlegge*)

No 3374. For two Royal Train workings in 1902 it was named *Britannia*, and had a large circular surround type of plate on the leading coupled wheel splashers, and a similar type of nameplate was used when the engine was employed in July 1902 for the special train conveying Lord Kitchener to London at the end of the South African War. It was evidently thought that the combined oval plate originally fitted to No 3377 was not prominent enough for such a notable occasion.

The twenty straight-framed Camels of 1900 had names that were nearly all connected with the West Country, and inevitably some of the topographical ones were fated to disappear in later years. The twenty engines were:

3353	Blasius	3363	One and All
3354	Bonaventura	3364	Pendragon
3355	Camelot	3365	Plymouth
3356	Dartmouth	3366	Restormel
3357	Smeaton	3367	St. Aubyn
3358	Godolphin	3368	Sir Stafford
3359	Kingsbridge	3369	Trelawney
3360	Launceston	3370	Tremayne
3361	Lyonesse	3371	Tregeagle
3362	Newlyn	3372	Torquay

All these locomotives had the oval combined plates on the cab sides, and had the standard domeless parallel boiler, with high raised Belpaire firebox. The last batch of Camels to be turned out new with this boiler was numbered 3413 to 3432, and entered service between December 1902 and May 1903. It was on this batch that new styles of nameplate were first seen. Nos 3413 to 3420 had the first form of what was to be the new standard type. Whatever the length of the actual name the plate itself was carried in a complete arc of a circle, from running plate to running plate, but because of

A Camel of 1903, No 3417 originally named *C. G. Mott* on a nameplate like that of *Bibby*. (British Railways)

the presence of the overhung springs the curved nameplate was spaced at some distance radially outwards from the splasher. The illustration of No 3416 *Bibby* shows this type very clearly. This batch was remarkable for the number of changes of name that took place in its history:

No	Original Name	Later Name
3413	Edward VII	—
3414	Albert Brassey	Albert Brassey
3415	Baldwin	Alfred Baldwin
3416	Bibby	Frank Bibby
3417	C. G. Mott	Charles Grey Mott*
3418	Earl of Cork	
3419	Evan Llewellyn	Evan Llewellyn
3420	Ernest Palmer	Sir Ernest Palmer †
3421	MacIver	David MacIver
3422	Sir John Llewellyn	Sir John Llewellyn
3423	Sir Massey	Sir Massey Lopes
3424	Sir Nigel	Sir N. Kingscote
3425	Sir W. H. Wills	Sir William Henry
3426	Walter Long	Walter Long
3427	Sir Watkin Wynn	Sir Watkin Wynn
3428	River Plym	River Plym
3429	Penzance	—
3430	River Tawe	River Tawe
3431	River Fal	River Fal
3432	River Yealm	River Yealm

*3417 was renamed a second time in 1923, becoming *Lord Mildmay of Flete*.
†3420 had its name transferred to 4-6-0 No 2975 in 1924.

The engines from 3421 onwards had the new standard nameplates from the time of construction. This is shown on the illustration of No 3419 after it had been so fitted.

The last batch of 4-4-0s to be built new with the domeless parallel boiler, the first Standard No 2, consisted of twenty Atbaras all named after cities of the British Empire. They had the new type of nameplate, extending from running

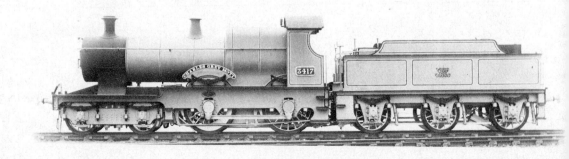

plate to running plate, but because of the larger diameter of the coupled wheels there was no need to have the spacer piece between nameplate and the top of the splasher. These twenty locomotives were:

3393	Auckland	3398	Colombo
3394	Adelaide	3399	Dunedin
3395	Aden	3400	Durban
3396	Brisbane	3401	Gibraltar
3397	Cape Town	3402	Halifax

'Pride of the station': a rebuilt 3521 class, with Camel boiler. *(British Railways)*

3403	Hobart	3408	Ophir
3404	Lyttleton	3409	Quebec
3405	Mauritius	3410	Sydney
3406	Melbourne	3411	St. Johns
3407	Malta	3412	Singapore

Cross-section of cylinders and bogie centre—Atbara class.

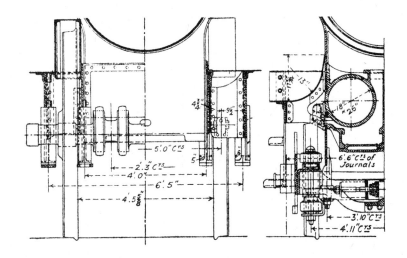

CHAPTER FIVE

ADVENT OF THE TAPER BOILER

In the paper 'Large Locomotive Boilers' presented by Churchward to the Institution of Mechanical Engineers on 16 February 1906, a paper as notable for the length and erudition of the discussion as for the original subject matter, the extent to which he had studied American practice was clearly apparent. The illustrations included detailed drawings of many very large boilers that embodied some coning of the barrel. The majority had wide, but round-topped, fireboxes of the Wootton type. Churchward said:

> Much more experience has been gained with the wide box in America than in this country, and, so far as the author has been able to ascertain, it has been found there that the poorer coals in large quantities can be burnt with much greater facility and economy in this type than in the narrow pattern. This advantage is offset to some extent by the fact that, when standing, there is considerable waste in the wide grates as compared with the narrow, and this is, of course, serious when goods trains are kept standing about, as is often the case here. This disadvantage has been found on the Great Western Railway, but no doubt careful design and fitting of ashpans will keep this waste within bounds.

A much more serious trouble has been found in the leaking of tubes in these boilers. This seems to be quite general, and the Master Mechanics' Association has a committee specially investigating this question with a view to finding a remedy. All methods of tube-expanding have been tried, and also much wider spacing, even up to and over 1 inch, without curing the trouble. The reduction of the depth of the firebox, in order to get a long box sloping over the trailing wheels of coupled engines, certainly increased the trouble from leakage of stays, but the alternative of a wide firebox entails a much heavier engine for most of the types, and then apparently tube-trouble is increased. The wide firebox evidently requires a higher standard of skill in the fireman, for unless the grate is kept well and evenly covered, there is a tendency to have an excess of air, reducing efficiency and increasing tube-trouble. With modern high pressures the temperature of evaporation is so much increased that the provision for circulation, which was sufficient for the lower pressures formerly used, is doubtless insufficient. Boilers in which this provision has been made have shown a very marked reduction in tube- and stay-troubles.

After drawing attention to illustrations in the paper, which showed that very liberal provision for water circulation had been provided in most of the American boilers, he went on:

> It is probable that in the wider boxes the main mass of the fire being so much nearer the tube-plate has a bad effect on the tubes, as the intensity of the temperature at the tube-plate must necessarily be much increased. The extra width of box has enabled the tubes to be put much too near the sides of the barrel. When this is done, the water to feed up the spaces between the tubes near the back tube-plate has to be drawn almost entirely from the

Atbara No 3405 *Mauritius*: the first GWR 4-4-0 to have a taper boiler. *(Locomotive Publishing Co)*

front of the barrel, and it is possible that in some cases the space left for this purpose is inadequate. It will probably be found that neglect of this consideration is the cause of three-fourths of the tube-trouble. In some of the boilers an effort has been made to provide for this upward circulation near the back tube-plate by leaving a space between the tubes and barrel from top to bottom, of a sectional area equal to the combined area of the vertical spaces between the tubes at all points, with a balance to provide for the water coming back from the front of the barrel to feed the water spaces of the firebox. There is no doubt that the upward draught of water through the spaces between the tubes for, say, two feet from the back tube-plate is very strong indeed, and in all probability this is enough to prevent the necessary feed of water down the spaces of the firebox unless ample area is given, so causing stay-trouble as well as tube-trouble.

It was with all these considerations in mind that he continued the development of his own boilers, and in relation to the present book it is important to appreciate that the earliest work on coned barrels took place on 4-4-0 locomotives. Unlike the Americans, who generally put the coning of their large boiler in the middle ring, Churchward began by coning the rearmost ring, and unlike the Americans also he retained the Belpaire type of firebox. He commented:

The gradual extension of the practice of making the top of the firebox and casing flat instead of round is noticeable. On the Great Western Railway less trouble has been experienced with the flat top firebox than with the round top, although no slingstays of any kind are used. The flat top has the important advantage of increasing the area of the water line at the hottest part of the boiler, and so materially contributes to the reduction of foaming. This, combined with the coned connection to the barrel, has enabled the dome, always a source of weakness, to be entirely dispensed with and drier steam obtained. The author some years ago made an experiment to settle this much-disputed point. Two identical engines and boilers were taken, one boiler having a dome in the usual position on the barrel, the other having no dome, the steam being taken by a pipe from the top of the flat firebox casing. The engine without the dome proved to be decidedly freer from priming than the other. The liberal dimension of two feet between the top of the firebox and the inside of the casing no doubt contributed to this satisfactory result. The coned barrel connection, in addition to providing a greater area of water line, also gives a larger steam capacity, and, by the larger diameter being arranged to coincide with the line of the firebox tube-plate, much more water-space at the sides of the tubes is possible. On consideration of the great intensity of temperature at the firebox plate as compared with that at the smokebox plate, the advantage of the arrangement is obvious.

The two boilers he referred to were not, with all respect, on identical engines, because one was the original *Bulldog* and the other was

Waterford, and they differed in their coupled wheel diameters. But following out the principles enunciated in the foregoing paragraph, he evolved what became known as the Standard No 4 boiler, and in its non-superheated form it was applied first to Atbara class No 3405 *Mauritius*. The boiler was coned for two-thirds of its length, increasing from 4ft 10¾in at the parallel front ring to no less than 5ft 6in at the firebox tube-plate. In one respect, however, the final form was not reached on *Mauritius*. The upper part of the firebox had vertical parallel sides, as on the Camels and standard Atbaras. Apart from this No 3405, reboilered thus in September 1902, was the true prototype of the most famous range of boilers in locomotive history. The basic details of the Atbara and Standard No 4 boilers were as follows:

	Atbara	No 4
TUBES:		
Number	277	350
Outside diameter, in	1⅞	1⅝
HEATING SURFACES:		
Tubes, sq ft	1540.18	1689.82
Firebox, sq ft	124.10	128.30
Total, sq ft	1664.28	1818.12
GRATE AREA:		
sq ft	21.28	20.56
BOILER PRESSURE:		
lb/sq in	180	200

No 3433, brand new, before being named, at Bath. (L & GRP)

It was possible to have a greater number of tubes on the No 4 not only because they were of smaller diameter, but because the forward ring of the barrel was 4ft 10¾in diameter outside against 4ft 5in in the parallel boiler of the Atbaras. It is interesting to find that Churchward increased the boiler pressure in the No 4 to 200lb/sq in and this brought the nominal tractive effort from 16,010lb to 17,790lb. The raising of the pressure caused some shaking of heads, particularly as some other railways were doing their best to get pressures down, in order to lessen boiler maintenance charges. It was therefore all the more interesting to hear what H. C. King, Locomotive Works Manager at Swindon, had to say about it:

The designs illustrated in the Paper [Churchward's classic of 1906] with the increased water surface, the conical barrel, and the improved area through which the water could very freely circulate, through the sides and back plates of the firebox, had produced for his company, whatever that pattern may have produced elsewhere, nothing but unqualified satisfaction. He could therefore state with the use of the higher pressures, the steady rise from 150lb to 165lb, then to 180lb, and now 200lb, with 225lb as a limit, had not produced that measure of increased difficulty which some people had anticipated would vary as the arithmetical ratio of the pressure. Of course there were difficulties—no one using locomotive boilers

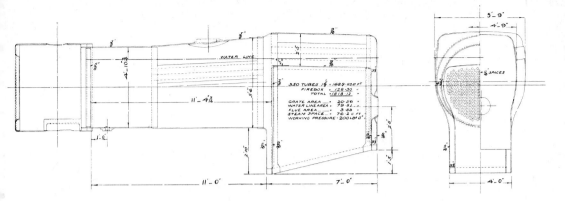

Longitudinal section of Standard No 4 boiler, as fitted to City class.

Cross-section through firebox showing curving sides.

was free from them—but there were no special difficulties incidental to the higher pressures. He was not going to say that that measure of satisfaction had been produced without constant and unremitting care on the part of all those in the boiler shop and in charge of the construction; everybody was aware that boilers were being built from which great things were expected, and he could say truthfully that the difficulties had not been proportional to the increased pressure.

I think that his last sentence is the crux of the whole matter: 'everyone was aware . . .' It was the same with the running inspectors on the footplate. Churchward was carrying the whole department—drawing office, works, and outdoor staff with him, in a combined, well-co-ordinated drive to 'great things'. It was on the City class of which No 3433 *City of Bath,* completed at Swindon in March 1903, was the first, that finality was reached in the shape of the Belpaire firebox, with the sides curved very slightly inwards towards the top and a much larger radius used in the transition from the sides to the flat top. Also, as will be seen from the drawing above, the top was not horizontal along the line of the boiler, but sloped down slightly towards the cab. In this respect Churchward was following American practice on many of the large boilers illustrated in his paper. Although it was the boiler that was the outstanding feature of *City of Bath*, it must be added that in these locomotives the Stroudley method of balancing was abandoned, and the outside cranks placed diametrically opposite to the inside, in the conventional way.

While *Mauritius* carried the first-ever taper

boiler produced at Swindon, the modified form on *City of Bath* was contemporaneous with the first tapered form of the Standard No 1, put on to Churchward's second express passenger 4-6-0, No 98. This had a half-coned boiler, of which a number of examples were built. *City of Bath* remained the only one of its class for two months and then, according to the Swindon records, the remaining nine engines of the class were turned out in May 1903. Quite apart from technicalities, the Cities were much finer-looking than the Atbaras. The larger boiler, with its centre line pitched three inches higher, and the tapered rear portion rising to meet the outline of the firebox, gave a balanced elegance that was absent in the angular functional aspects of the Atbaras. In a further respect opinions may differ, but I think they looked their best with the tapered cast iron chimneys, especially those with the raised cowl at the front. The later large-diameter 'copper tops' and such additions as top feed, certainly gave them a 'standard' appearance, but I prefer the older version.

There were some curiosities about the naming. As will be seen from this list the first nine were neatly in alphabetical order, and it looked as though Exeter had been forgotten and was put in at the last minute! Then there is the inclusion of Winchester, reached only by a sparsely used branch line, and Worcester omitted. It looks as though No 3442 was to have been *City of Worcester* and that the name was discarded in favour of *City of Exeter*. The GWR already had one of the 7ft 8in singles named simply *Worcester*, so presumably honour was satisfied. The class, as completed, was as detailed overleaf.

No 3436 *City of Chester* in original condition.
(Locomotive Publishing Co)

3433   *City of Bath*
3434   *City of Birmingham*
3435   *City of Bristol*
3436   *City of Chester*
3437   *City of Gloucester*
3438   *City of Hereford*
3439   *City of London*
3440   *City of Truro*
3441   *City of Winchester*
3442   *City of Exeter*

1903 was a great year for the Locomotive Department of the GWR. Quite apart from the successful introduction of the finalised form of taper boiler, it saw the commissioning of Churchward's famous dynamometer car. One of the first jobs carried out with it was a full-dress trial of one of the Cities on 27 July 1903, between Taunton and Exeter. It seemed as if an attempt to determine the 'all-out' capacity of these locomotives was made. I was able to study the actual dynamometer car record, and from it I have prepared the accompanying log. The ascent of the steepest part of the Wellington bank was quite exceptional for the period. The load would have been considered on the heavy side for a top-class Great Western express of that period, and for the speed not to have fallen

below 40mph over the last mile to Whiteball Tunnel involved some very hard work. In fact, the cylinders were very definitely 'beating the boiler'. After the immediate start from Taunton No 3435 was worked in 38 per cent cut-off, with regulator three-quarters full open, to Wellington. This had brought the boiler pressure down from the rated 200 to 160lb/sq in. Here the engine was exerting a drawbar pull of no less than 2.2 tons, at 53mph. On the final ascent, when one mile short of the tunnel entrance (milepost 172), cut-off was advanced to 48 per cent and although boiler pressure fell still further, to 150lb/sq in, the 1 in 80 gradient was topped at 38mph, and on the mile at 1 in 127 through the tunnel the speed dropped no more than 1mph. The actual drawbar pull on entering the tunnel was no less than three tons, and the equivalent drawbar horsepower, on level track, no less than 920. This was an outstanding effort at such a speed as 38mph, but it was clear that it could not be sustained for long.

For test purposes a stop was made at Tiverton Junction, prior to which there had been a fast descent from Whiteball. From the restart the locomotive was worked in 26 per cent cut-off and regulator one-half open, and made fast time down the gently falling gradient from Cullompton to the outskirts of Exeter. When *City of Truro* was restored to working condition in 1957, and I had the pleasure of riding on the

DYNAMOMETER CAR TEST RUN : 27 July 1903
No 3435 *City of Bristol*
Load: 240 tons

Distance Miles			Actual min sec		Average speeds mph
0.0	TAUNTON YARD		0	00	—
0.8	Milepost	164	2	40	—
1.8	''	165	4	08	40.9
2.8	''	166	5	19	50.7
3.8	''	167	6	28	52.2
4.8	''	168	7	36	53.0
5.8	''	169	8	44	53.0
6.8	''	170	9	52	53.0
7.8	''	171	10	09	53.7
8.3	''	171 1/2	10	44	51.5
8.8	''	172	11	23	46.2
9.3	''	172 1/2	12	06	41.9
9.8	''	173	12	51	40.0
10.8	''	174 (Whiteball)	14	27	37.5
11.8	''	175	15	40	49.3
12.8	''	176	16	35	65.4
13.8	''	177	17	24	73.5
14.8	''	178	18	12	75.0
15.8	Tiverton Junc (179)		20	00	—
1.0	Milepost	180	3	01	—
2.0	''	181	4	15	48.7
3.0	''	182	5	15	60.0
4.0	''	183	6	12	63.2
5.0	''	184	7	06	66.7
6.0	''	185	7	58	69.2
7.0	''	186	8	51	67.9
8.0	''	187	9	44	67.9
9.0	''	188	10	34	72.0
10.0	''	189	11	24	72.0
12.0	''	191	13	03	73.5
14.9	EXETER		16	30	—

footplate, I noted that the locomotive ran beautifully in 26 per cent cut-off, though at that time it was superheated and the original slide valves had been replaced by piston valves. That, however, is a later part of the present story. In 1903 Churchward's master plan for locomotive modernisation on the GWR was getting into its stride, but while the first 4-6-0s were in service

and the de Glehn compound Atlantic *La France* had arrived and was doing first-class work, Churchward was well enough aware that for several years the Atbaras and Cities would be the backbone of the motive power stud, and there was every reason to have a clear assessment of their maximum capacity. The dynamometer car test with *City of Bristol* in July 1903 certainly gave the answer.

The stud of 4-4-0 locomotives with the Standard No 4 boiler was augmented between November 1903 and March 1910 by the rebuilding of seventeen Badmintons and nine Atbaras. All the latter were of the British Empire series, and were numbered consecutively 3400 to 3409, this group including *Mauritius*. These ten remained Cities for the rest of their existence, but the conversion of the Badmintons was transient. As the case histories show that these seventeen later received Standard No 2 boilers. The only three Badmintons not to receive No 4 boilers were *Monarch*, *Charles Mortimer* and *Oxford*. At this stage the Badmintons had their frames strengthened, as can be seen by the riveting evident on the photograph of *Bessborough* below. It is interesting to recall that the first of these locomotives to have the Standard No 4 boiler was *Waterford*, which from November 1903 carried the original and ultimately unique boiler for almost five years.

The other boiler that was unique among Swindon productions was that put on to No 3297 *Earl Cawdor* in July 1903, and which was quite

A Badminton rebuilt with a Standard No 4 boiler: No 3295 *Bessborough. (British Railways)*

The Badminton rebuilt with the Wright type of boiler:
No 3297 *Earl Cawdor*. (British Railways)

apart from the general line of development
being pursued by Churchward at that time. Not
long previously F. G. Wright had been
appointed Chief Assistant to the Chief
Mechanical Engineer, a post that he held for the
ensuing nineteen years. He had previously been
Locomotive Works Manager, and was deeply
concerned in boiler development. It became
known that he was in some way connected with
the rebuilding of the *Earl Cawdor*, but there has
been some confusion of thought as to just how
this had taken place. H. Holcroft has written:

Apparently he was influenced by the
performance of McIntosh's big boiler engines
on the Caledonian, and he wanted to go one
better. The idea was evidently that a large
storage of hot water would act as a reservoir
and assist engines on an undulating profile,
and he was permitted to try it out.

But Wright himself gave the real clue in his
contribution to the discussion on Churchward's
paper of 1906:

Another point, which he did not quite see how
they were to overcome, was that in very large

boilers the engineers had been obliged to
decrease the depth of the firebox. With the
older class of boiler, having deeper fireboxes,
the trouble was not experienced with the
stays, which has taken place since the depth
has been decreased, necessitating the boiler
being fired with a comparatively thin fire, and
the area of the depth of the firebox in contact
with the fire being very much reduced. The
lengthening of the firebox did not counteract
this, as the depth was not increased where the
heat was being applied to generate steam;
that is, a boiler with a firebox, say, 3 feet deep,
had a certain area in contact with the fire, but
if this were reduced, say, to 18 inches deep,
the area had been reduced by half.

In comparing the drawing of the boiler of *Earl
Cawdor* with that of the Standard No 4 one can
see at once how Wright was attempting to meet
the objection he had postulated. The boiler of
Earl Cawdor was strikingly similar to that of the
LNWR Precursors, in the very deep firebox and
horizontal grate set between the axles of the
coupled wheels—though so far as dates were
concerned *Earl Cawdor* preceded *Precursor* by
about nine months. The feature of this special
boiler was not so much to provide a reservoir for

Longitudinal section of the Cawdor boiler.   Cross-section

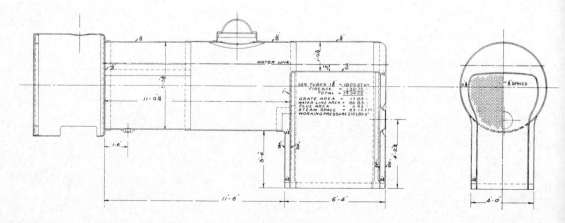

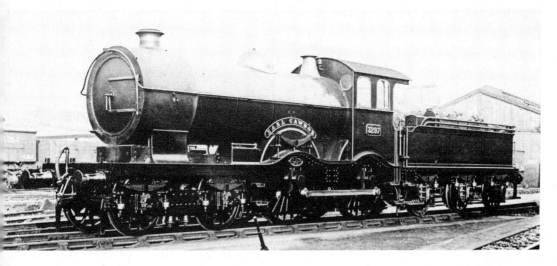

Earl Cawdor with the Wright type boiler, at Westbourne Park. *(L & GRP)*

not water as a reservoir for steam, because the steam space was 85.13cu ft against the admittedly generous 76.2cu ft of the Standard No 4. The respective water line areas were 86.85sq ft (*Earl Cawdor*) and 79.81sq ft (Standard No 4). The big difference lay in the grates, with respective areas of 17.85 and 20.56sq ft. Wright undoubtedly intended his boiler to be fed from a fairly thick fire, more in the North Western style. The tube arrangements were much the same, and there was plenty of space on *Earl Cawdor* for circulation of water past the tubes at the firebox end. An interesting point about Wright's boiler was that the working pressure was still higher, at 210 lb/sq in. The locomotive ran with this boiler for three years, and then had a Standard No 4 substituted.

It was not surprising that the appearance of this engine, so early in the Churchward regime should have given rise to much surprise and speculation. At the time it first took the road in July 1903, there were only the eleven taper-boiler 4-4-0s of the City class running, together with the three experimental 4-6-0s, Nos 100, 98, 171, and the de Glehn compound 4-4-2 No 102 *La France*. Not enough was known of what was planned at Swindon to place the reboilered *Earl Cawdor* as an engine by itself. The fact that it had a large side-window cab in the North Eastern style merely increased the speculation. That most scholarly and devoted of Great Western enthusiasts, the late J. N. Maskelyne, has written:

I remember that when a photograph of the rebuilt engine appeared in *The Locomotive*

No 3310 *Waterford*, rebuilt with Standard No 4 boiler, but retaining the original cab. *(L & GRP)*

The 'comedian among railway engines': rebuilt No 3297 *Earl Cawdor* at Reading. *(L & GRP)*

Magazine on 10 October 1903, a small group of schoolboys—myself included—dissolved into fits of laughter! That absurd dome— which, incidentally, was a remarkable

A Camel of 1904, No 3466 *Barbados* with half-cone No 2 boiler, and later standard type of nameplate. *(British Railways)*

anticipation of the 'tin hat' that became such a familiar item of the military sartorial outfit, 40 years later—perched on the huge boiler; that tremendous smokebox surmounted by a squat chimney, and that great cab with its elongated roof and large double side windows, together with the general effect of obesity and bloatedness, were too much for us. We could not look at that photograph without merriment; but we were young, not one of us having entered his teens, and it

The height of 4-4-0 elegance: Atbara No 3408 *Ophir* rebuilt with Standard No 4 boiler, and lipped cast-iron chimney. *(British Railways)*

meant that our sense of the ridiculous was apt to overflow at the least provocation.

But Maskelyne's interest, however frivolous at the time, led to about the only solid piece of information about the performance of the engine during the time it carried Wright's boiler. At the preparatory school he then attended there was a master interested in locomotives, and having been shown that photograph he agreed to take a small party of boys to Paddington in the hopes of seeing this 'comedian among railway engines'. They were not disappointed, because *Earl Cawdor* came in with an Ocean Mail special. I quote Maskelyne again: 'Our guide had a chat with the driver, who did not seem to think much of the engine; he said she ought to be able to pull a house down, but she wanted far more coaxing than any other engine he had driven.' In fact it did very little first-class express work, and one of its later turns was a heavy train of milk empties that used to run each afternoon from Kensington (Addison Road) to Swindon.

CHAPTER SIX

THE *CITIES* AND THE OCEAN MAILS

No class of British express passenger loco-motives—not even the Gresley A4 Pacifics of the LNER—had a more spectacular début than the Great Western Cities. I have explained in the previous chapter how they had the important role of caretaker during the earlier stages of Churchward's great programme of develop-ment, but it was a role they played so brilliantly that some at least among contemporary observers wondered if there was really any need to build larger and more expensive locomotives. The doubts were not absent from the Board Table at Paddington. *City of Bath* took the road at the same time as Churchward's first taper-boilered 4-6-0 No 98, and later in that same momentous year of 1903 *La France* arrived from Alfred de Glehn's works, in Belfort. For a time these huge new locomotives worked turn and turn about with the Cities. There did seem however a strong disposition to use the 4-4-0s when an assignment of very special importance arose. This was certainly the case on 14 July 1903, when the Prince and Princess of Wales, afterwards King George V and Queen Mary, were to pay a visit to Cornwall. Not being the reigning monarch the full Royal Train was not called for, and three saloons were attached to the first portion of the ordinary 10.40am Cornishman, and arrangements made to run this first portion non-stop to Plymouth.

The Great Western authorities evidently intended from the very outset to make something of a gala occasion of it, for they invited Rous-Marten and the Rev W. J. Scott to travel in that part of the train available to the public. Furthermore, the story goes that someone in very high quarters asked for 'a good run', with the result that the train arrived in Plymouth 36¼ minutes ahead of time! One might have thought that for an occasion like that, when the working of the train was obviously to be a matter of prestige that one of Churchward's latest 'big' engines would have been put on to the job. But no; the engine was *City of Bath* with the same driver, Burden, of Westbourne Park shed, who had done so well with the Royal special of 1902, then with the Atbara class 4-4-0 *Baden Powell* alias *Britannia*. In July 1903 the load was 130 tons, an easy one from the viewpoint of power output, but important seeing that the load was to be conveyed non-stop to Plymouth, and that the South Devon banks had to be tackled after the engine had been at work for more than three hours. It is interesting in that connection to compare the loads taken by the City class, particularly in the Ocean Mail 'racing' of 1904 with the stipulated loads for the later express locomotives of the GWR:

Locomotive class	Nominal tractive effort lb	Tonnage, South Devon line	Ratio: load (lb) to tractive effort (lb)
City	17,790	150	16.8
Star	27,800	288	23.2
King	40,300	360	20.0

The foregoing, of course, compares ordinary service with special conditions, and in ordinary working the 4-4-0 engines took loads up to 200

No 3433 *City of Bath* carrying the insignia of the Prince of Wales at Laira shed, after the record run of 14 July 1903. *(P. H. Counsell)*

tons without assistance, in which case the ratio would be 22.4, or practically equal to that of the Stars.

To revert to the record run of 14 July 1903, however, of which a very complete log, with all the average speeds, is given on page 68, it clearly represented the ideal performance of the locomotive. Had there been any attempt at forcing the pace, it would have been reflected in fluctuation in steam pressure, and consequently see-sawing up and down of the speed. But if one looks at the long distance averages, such as that of 71.3mph from Southall to Swindon, and of 74.4mph from Nailsea to Durston, the steadiness of the running is emphasised. Also it can be seen that 67¾ miles were covered in the first hour from Paddington, 135½ miles in two hours, and 200¼ miles in three hours—the last two figures representing average speeds of 67.7 and 66.8mph from the dead start. The speed of the locomotive with this load, on level track, seemed to be 75 to 77mph, while the downhill speeds of 87½mph on Dauntsey incline, and 83½mph from Flax Bourton were merely incidental. There was no need to press the locomotive for a high minimum speed up the Wellington bank,

though Rous-Marten claimed that the speed there did not fall below 50mph. Even faster time might have been made to Exeter had not the engine been eased downhill from Whiteball, out of consideration for the Royal party which was then at lunch.

There was, however, no dawdling between Exeter and Plymouth, to make a time of only 61 minutes 1 second between those stations. There must have been some smart accelerations between the various speed restrictions to run between Exeter and Newton Abbot in 23 minutes 17 seconds and then some remarkable climbing of the South Devon banks followed. Rous-Marten gives the minimum speeds as 32mph up Dainton bank, and 36mph up Rattery. While the intermittent demands for steam after Exeter had been passed markedly reduced the general effort required from the engine, it is evident from these robust climbs that things were still in good shape on the footplate after three hours of continuous high-speed running, and on arrival

GWR 10.40am PADDINGTON-PLYMOUTH
with Royal Saloons attached. 14 July 1903
No 3433 *City of Bath*
Load: 130 tons gross

Distance Miles		Actual min sec	Average speeds mph
0.0	PADDINGTON	0 00	–
1.3	Westbourne Park	2 47	–
5.7	Ealing Broadway	7 32	53.7
9.1	Southall	10 35	66.9
13.2	West Drayton	14 13	67.7
16.2	Langley	16 42	72.4
18.5	SLOUGH	18 35	73.3
24.2	Maidenhead	23 26	70.5
31.0	Twyford	29 14	70.3
36.0	READING	33 26	71.5
38.7	Tilehurst	35 43	70.9
41.5	Pangbourne	38 07	72.4
44.8	Goring	40 47	71.9
48.5	Cholsey	43 50	72.8
53.1	DIDCOT	47 33	74.4
60.4	Wantage Road	53 40	71.6
66.5	Uffington	58 56	69.5
71.6	Shrivenham	63 12	71.8
77.3	SWINDON	68 01	71.1
82.9	Wootton Bassett	72 44	71.3
87.7	Dauntsey	76 31	76.0
94.0	CHIPPENHAM	81 10	81.3
98.3	Corsham	84 54	68.8
101.9	Box	87 41	77.4
104.6	Bathampton	89 55	72.4
106.9	BATH	92 02*	62.8
111.4	Saltford	96 42	57.4
113.8	Keynsham	98 44	70.6
117.0	*Bristol East Depot*	101 52*	61.2
118.7	*Pylle Hill Junc*	104 42*	27.6
124.0	Flax Bourton	110 46	52.6
130.0	Yatton	115 45	72.2
142.2	Brent Knoll	125 24	76.0
145.0	Highbridge	127 36	76.4
151.3	Bridgwater	132 45	73.4
162.8	TAUNTON	142 39	69.7
164.8	Norton Fitzwarren	144 58	52.0
169.9	Wellington	150 03	60.2
173.7	*Whiteball Box*	154 27	51.8
178.7	Tiverton Junc	158 58	66.5
181.0	Cullompton	160 57	69.6
190.2	Stoke Canon	169 12	66.9
193.6	EXETER	172 34*	60.8
198.3	Exminster	178 32	47.2
202.1	Starcross	181 54	67.6
205.8	Dawlish	185 32*	60.9
208.6	Teignmouth	190 15*	35.4
213.8	NEWTON ABBOT	195 51*	55.7
217.7	*Dainton Box*	201 28	40.6
222.5	Totnes	206 46	54.4
227.0	*Rattery Box*	213 24	40.7
229.3	Brent	216 12	49.3
231.5	Wrangaton	218 45	51.7
238.9	*Hemerdon Box*	226 24	58.0
241.6	Plympton	228 54	64.8
245.6	PLYMOUTH (North Road)	233 35	–

Severe speed restrictions marked *
Slight check through Taunton

at Plymouth in 233½ minutes from Paddington, an altogether unprecedented feat of performance had been achieved, in making a start-to-stop average speed of 63.2mph over such a distance as 246 miles. That it had been done with a semi-Royal Train added to the unusual and epoch-marking nature of the run. *City of Bath* was firmly established as the veritable 'pride of the line'; and it only needed the dynamometer car test with *City of Bristol* described in the previous chapter to show another and equally valuable facet of performance of the new engines.

Railway enthusiasts knew nothing of the test run, but the record times made with the semi-Royal *Cornishman* set going a host of conjectures as to how this kind of speed might be applied to other railway routes in Great Britain. The Rev. W. J. Scott, for example, pictured the LNWR reaching Preston in 3 hours 11 minutes from Euston; the Great Northern getting to York in 2 hours 48 minutes, and the North Eastern running from York to Edinburgh in 3 hours 6 minutes. But the world had to wait until the Spring of 1904 for further demonstrations of what the City class could do. It is true that the first two-hour trains between Paddington and Bristol were put on in August 1903, but these belong to the ordinary rather

than to the exceptional ranges of performance. It was the increasingly severe competition with the London & South Western Railway for the Ocean Mail traffic from Plymouth to London that put the City class locomotives into banner headlines. It was the increasing interest of the South Western, and the installation of greatly improved passenger facilities at Stonehouse Pool quay that really touched off the contest—a contest for which the Great Western was not unprepared! Until then the Great Western had enjoyed a monopoly of the inward-bound American traffic, and was quietly delighting in a covert rivalry with the London & North Western who worked in partnership with the Cunard and White Star liners sailing via Liverpool. By 1903 the crack German liners which had recently wrested the Blue Riband of the Atlantic crossing from Great Britain began calling at Plymouth, and this saved a day in the journey time from New York to London, as compared with the runs of the British liners berthing at Liverpool, and served by LNWR specials to Euston.

In 1903 the normal procedure was for West of England expresses to change engines at Exeter, with Camels or Dukes replacing the Atbaras or 4-2-2s that had worked down from Bristol, or through from Paddington on the few non-stop trains. When the Ocean Mail contest began in

No 3442 *City of Exeter,* maker of several notable Ocean Mail runs.

earnest on 9 April 1904, Camel class 4-4-0, No 3452 *Wolverhampton* worked the train from Millbay Crossing to Exeter, not very brilliantly, in seventy-two minutes for the 52.9 miles. It was then replaced by *City of Exeter*, which up to 7 May featured on some part of every single mail run but one. No 3442 was obviously a favourite down in the West Country, and its début on 9 April 1904 was a brilliant one, running the five-coach train over the 75.6 miles from Exeter to Bristol (Temple Meads) in sixty-six minutes. Nine days later it worked through from Plymouth non-stop to Bristol, but although doing better than the Camel over the South Devon line, and passing Exeter in sixty-eight minutes it strangely enough did not do so well on to Bristol, taking 70½ minutes pass-to-stop. On 23 April, again with *City of Exeter*, a much faster time was made over the South Devon line, passing Newton Abbot in forty-one minutes, but

OCEAN MAIL SPECIAL 9 April 1904
No 3442 *City of Exeter*
Load: 5 vans; 150 tons full

Distance Miles		Actual min sec		Average speed mph
0.0	EXETER	0	00	—
1.3	*Cowley Bridge Junc*	2	40	—
14.9	Tiverton Junc	15	02	66.0
19.9	*Whiteball Box*	19	30	67.1
23.7	Wellington	23	02	64.7
30.8	TAUNTON	27	55	87.1
42.3	Bridgwater	36	42	78.5
55.9	*Uphill Junc*	47	24	76.3
63.6	Yatton	53	35	74.7
74.5	Bedminster	62	30	73.4
75.6	BRISTOL (Temple Meads)	65	24	—

some of the advantage of this was subsequently lost, and the time to Bristol was 136 minutes. On 30 April there were the makings of a real record, for Newton Abbot was passed in no more than thirty-seven minutes. Something then went amiss with the engine, which had to come off at Exeter. The load was five vans, or about 150 tons, on the first three occasions, and one less on the fourth. On 9 April the Rev. W. J. Scott was an invited guest, and he logged the run in detail. It included some performance of outstanding merit, as revealed by the accompanying log. On the easier part of the ascent to Whiteball the speed was between 71 and 72mph, and after taking the steeper pitch from Cullompton to Tiverton Junction, the maximum of 72mph was renewed before tackling the final two miles at 1 in 115 up to Whiteball Summit. Here Scott clocked a minimum of 60mph. Then, although the engine seems to have been restrained a little down the steepest part of the Wellington bank, there was clearly some very fast running afterwards to make an average speed of 87.1mph from Wellington to Taunton. The run concluded with what could be called a characteristic piece of City running—an average of 77.5mph over the 43.7 miles from Taunton to Bedminster. On another run logged some little time afterwards by Rous-Marten, to which more detailed reference will subsequently be made, the time from Whiteball to Taunton was exactly the same, and he claimed a maximum speed of

OCEAN MAILS : PLYMOUTH-LONDON
THROUGH LOCOMOTIVES

Locomotive No. Locomotive Name:		3437 *City of* *Gloucester*	3442 *City of* *Exeter*	City Class
Load vans:				
	Plymouth-Bristol	5	5	5
	Bristol-Paddington	3	3	3
Distance *Miles*		*Time* *min*	*Time* *min*	*Time* *min*
0.0	Millbay Crossing	0	0	0
24.0	Totnes	28	30	—
32.7	Newton Abbot	37	40	—
52.9	Exeter	58	61	61 1/4
83.7	Taunton	88	90	89 1/2
95.2	Bridgwater	99	100	—
127.8	Pylle Hill Junc	128	128	—
128.5	Temple Meads	—	—	128 1/4
41.4	Swindon	39	41 1/2	41 1/4
65.6	Didcot	60	63 1/2	63
82.7	Reading	74 1/2	77 1/2	77 1/4
118.7	Paddington	106	110 1/2	109 1/2
Overall time		3hr 56min	4hr 1min	4hr 0min

95½mph. On the non-stop runs made by *City of Exeter* on 18 April and 23 April, it is evident that the running was not so hard, but that on 30 April must have involved some tremendous work over the South Devon line.

Then, as the competition began to work up to its climax there were two runs on which one City class engine worked through from Plymouth to Paddington, pausing no more than briefly at Pylle Hill Junction to detach the vans carrying the North of England mails. On 30 April when

No 3433 *City of Bath* at Westbourne Park shed. *(Locomotive Publishing Co)*

City of Exeter had made such a vigorous start the overall time had for the first time been brought below four hours, though engines had to be changed both at Exeter and Pylle Hill; but on that occasion the honours east of Exeter rest with the 7ft 8in 4-2-2s that ran the train. A supplementary table shows the journal times of the runs made by *City of Gloucester* on 2 May and *City of Exeter* once again, on 7 May. With a load of five vans, against four, *City of Gloucester* made very fast time to Exeter, particularly round the coastal stretch from Newton Abbot—20.2 miles in twenty-one minutes!—but was eased down a little afterwards. *City of Exeter* was three minutes slower in passing Newton Abbot, but gradually caught up to make a dead heat of it into Pylle Hill. Both locomotives then made some fast running east of Swindon, with respective average speeds of 69.2 and 65.5mph on to Didcot; 70.8 and 73.3mph from there to Reading, and concluding averages, pass to stop, of 68.6 and 65.5mph from Reading to Paddington. In this table I have also put the time made by an anonymous City class engine, logged by Rous-Marten, on which the details were not released until 1906. On this run the uphill speeds were given as 25½mph on Hemerdon bank, 37½mph at Dainton, and 56¼mph at Whiteball. This was followed by the maximum of 95½mph previously quoted.

It was in 1906 that news came of the first non-stop runs from Millbay Crossing to Paddington with the Ocean Mails, and this involved slipping the two vans containing the North Country mails at Bedminster. The usual

'Official' photograph of *City of Truro,* actually that of 3433 skilfully 'doctored' photographically. *(British Railways)*

formation then consisted of three of the large elliptical-roofed stowage vans and a TPO sorting van at the rear. The sorting was all finished by the time Bristol was neared and the TPO was one of the two vehicles slipped. Schedule time for the non-stop run was four hours exactly, but at that time 4-6-0 locomotives were also being used on those trains.

Every other facet in the working of the Ocean Mails is however subjugated to the 'Record of Records' run on 9 May 1904, when *City of Truro* was the engine from Plymouth to Bristol. Although there were several denials afterwards that this run was made other than in the course of ordinary business, one can have every suspicion that it was otherwise! For one thing, the Assistant Superintendent of the Line, Charles Aldington, travelled on the train; although it was by that time nothing unusual for Rous-Marten to be invited (he had, in fact, been on the train two days earlier, when *City of Exeter* worked through to Paddington) it was unusual for the representative of a prominent West Country daily newspaper, the *Western Daily Mercury,* also to be invited. I have a cutting of the very interesting and *accurate* account that appeared in that newspaper the very next morning. Rous-Marten wrote two articles immediately. There was a long account, with a complete log, that was published in *The Engineer* of 20 May 1904, and a shorter one, obviously rushed through for publication in the June 1904 issue of *The Railway Magazine.*

Before discussing the actual details of the running, it is interesting to recall once again that it was the intention, if possible, to work through to London with the one engine. It had become the practice to have top-link engines standing by at Exeter and elsewhere in case one was needed in a hurry, as it had been at Exeter on 30 April,

but there were other considerations on 9 May. After noting the arrival at Pylle Hill Junction, Rous-Marten continued:

Up to this point the engine *City of Truro,* had performed in a manner that left nothing to be desired. She arrived in excellent trim, with all her bearings and parts perfectly cool, and she was in every way fit for the remaining run of 118½ miles to London. But the journey of 246¾ miles at such speeds, and over such gradients, consumes a large quantity of coal, and when we stopped at Pylle Hill, although we had eased down slightly during the last few miles, it became evident that the inroad into our fuel supply had been very heavy. It was possible that what remained might carry us through to London all right without necessitating any economy; but, on the other hand, there was a possibility of shortage, and as it seemed inadvisable to incur even the slightest risk of such a contingency as delay for this reason, it was decided, after brief consultation, to change engines.

Now the Cities as built had the same tenders as the Atbaras, with a water capacity of three thousand gallons, and four tons of coal. The Atbaras in the link at Westbourne Park shed were averaging about 32lb of coal per mile, though this would of course cover everything, including lighting-up, standing-by, and so on. The actual consumption on a long through run would have been considerably less, probably twenty-seven to 30lb per mile. Even at the higher figure a load of four tons on the tender at Plymouth should have given plenty for a 246¾ mile run, likely to take 3¼ tons, but there was no

GWR: OCEAN MAIL — 9 MAY 1904
No 3440 *City of Truro*
Load: 5 vans; 148 tons loaded

Distance Miles		Actual min sec	Average speed mph
0.0	MILLBAY CROSSING	0 00	—
0.9	PLYMOUTH (North Rd.)	3 07	17.3
1.2	Mutley	3 36	37.2
4.9	Plympton	7 31	55.2
7.6	*Hemerdon Box*	11 54	36.9
9.3	Cornwood	14 05	46.6
11.7	Ivybridge	16 29	60.0
15.0	Wrangaton	19 48	59.8
17.2	Brent	21 43	68.8
24.0	Totnes	27 39	68.8
28.8	*Dainton Box*	32 40	57.5
32.7	NEWTON ABBOT	36 42	58.0
37.9	Teignmouth	41 59	59.0
40.7	Dawlish	45 54	42.9
44.4	Starcross	50 14	51.2
—		pws	—
48.2	Exminster	54 09	58.3
52.1	Exeter St. Thomas's	57 49	63.8
52.9	EXETER (St. David's)	59 02	39.5
56.4	Stoke Canon	62 54	54.4
60.1	Silverton	66 26	62.9
61.3	Hele	67 33	64.5
65.5	Cullompton	71 13	68.8
67.8	Tiverton Junc	73 32	59.8
72.1	Burlescombe	77 43	61.6
72.8	*Whiteball Box*	78 31	53.5
73.8	*Milepost 173*	79 26	65.7
74.8	*Milepost 172*	80 08	85.7
75.8	*Milepost 171*	80 45 1/2	96.0
—		brakes	
76.6	Wellington	81 18	89.2
81.7	Norton Fitzwarren	85 19	76.5
83.7	TAUNTON	86 51	78.2
89.5	Durston	91 42	71.6
95.2	Bridgwater	96 10	76.5
101.5	Highbridge	101 09	75.7
116.5	Yatton	113 01	75.9
122.5	Flax Bourton	118 11	69.7
127.4	Bedminster	122 19	70.9
127.8	PYLLE HILL JUNC	123 19	—

doubt the engines of the Ocean Mail trains were being worked considerably harder than the Atbaras at Westbourne Park, and one can sympathise with Inspector Flewellyn in taking a fresh engine at Bristol on this very special occasion. The utterly brilliant run made by the relief engine *Duke of Connaught* led to comparisons being made between coupled and single engines on the fast running stretches east of Swindon, with the single, hauling four vans going from Swindon to Paddington in just under

City of Truro at Exeter, about the time of the record Ocean Mail run. *(O. S. Nock collection)*

the hour, whereas *City of Gloucester* and *City of Exeter*, each hauling three vans took sixty-seven and sixty-nine minutes respectively. But these engines had both worked through from Plymouth, having made very fast time to Pylle Hill, and it may well be that their crews were having to conserve their coal supply in the later stages of the runs.

I now come to the detailed analysis of the run of 9 May. In bare outline it was very little faster than that of *City of Gloucester* on 2 May, as far as Newton Abbot, with times of 27 minutes 39 seconds to Totnes, and 36 minutes 42 seconds to Newton Abbot itself, where Rous-Marten

reported no more than a 'slight slack'. But the restrictions round the coastal section were evidently taken more cautiously by *City of Truro*, for its time to Exeter was a minute **more** than that of *City of Gloucester*. Furthermore, on 30 April *City of Exeter* had tied with these times to Totnes and Newton Abbot, and stopped at Exeter in the level hour. From this it is evident that on 9 May *City of Truro* was making what could be described as the standard performance for the City class over the South Devon line. Rous-Marten's detailed log shows how it was done, intermediately. The speeds must have involved some very lively travelling. To get a good run at Hemerdon bank, speed was worked up to 70mph through Plympton, following which the minimum speed on the 1 in 41 was 27mph. Speeds of 62 to 65mph were reported on the rising length to Wrangaton, but the hair-raising '77mph down Rattery Incline' contained in one subsequent account, was actually a brief dash at 75-77mph on the relatively straight length between the Brent S-curves and the top of the Rattery bank—a relatively safe proposition. The very steep descents from Rattery to Totnes, and Dainton Tunnel to Aller Junction were made quite cautiously.

The next stage for analysis is the climb from Exeter to Whiteball summit, and here a most important comparison can be made with the run of 9 April, made by *City of Exeter* from a dead start in St. David's station. It is true that non-stopping trains were then required to slow to walking pace in passing through, but *City of Exeter* from the dead start took only 15 minutes 2 seconds to pass Tiverton Junction against the 14 minutes 30 seconds of *City of Truro*. Furthermore, over the final stage the honours undoubtedly rest with the earlier run. The respective times from Tiverton Junction to the Whiteball box, just five miles, were 4 minutes 28 seconds and 4 minutes 59 seconds, respective averages of 67.1 and 60.1mph. So, up to this point *City of Truro* was running generally up to the best standards of its sister engines—not breaking records.

Then came the descent from Whiteball to Taunton, over which so much argument, conjecture, and controversy has arisen, since 1930, when *City of Truro* was set aside to become a cherished museum piece. In his article in *The Engineer* of 20 May 1904, Rous-Marten wrote:

Here the speed was very high, and, as I have had occasion to note in other cases, the running was the smoothest and steadiest of the whole journey. The motion resembled a sliding along the smoothest ice, and not the slightest oscillation could be detected in the van where I made my observations. It is difficult to calculate or even to conjecture what maximum might ultimately have been attained, had the course from Whiteball to Taunton been unimpeded, but, most luckily, the sheer stupidity of three platelayers baulked us at this interesting point, beside placing themselves in the most imminent peril. They coolly and doggedly remained on the up line, right in the middle of the 4ft way, although previously warned to be careful, and additionally warned by the protracted whistle of the engine. . . .

In the meantime, as we know all too well, Rous-Marten had clocked a quarter-mile in 8.8 seconds—102.3mph No doubt Charles Aldington learned very soon about this, and asked him to keep it 'under his hat' for the time being. But the correspondent of the *Western Daily Mercury* was also in the secret, and apparently no similar request was made to him, for the very next morning his account included the following:

Five minutes were occupied between Wellington and Taunton (10.50am) the speed now being terrific, and at times being between ninety-nine and a hundred miles an hour. Nine minutes sufficed for the 11½ miles to Bridgwater which was left behind at 10.59am, the rate between these places being no less than 77.07 miles an hour. . . .

The actual times, as will be seen from Rous-Marten's original log were 5 minutes 13 seconds and 9 minutes 23 seconds. In several previous books* I have gone to some length in explaining my acceptance of a maximum speed of at least 100mph on behalf of *City of Truro*, though actually this is the only point in its historic run when superiority was shown over other members of the class. A summary of the best times made in April and May 1904 with the Ocean Mails shows the following:

PLYMOUTH (Millbay Crossing)

To:	Minutes	Locomotive
Newton Abbot	36 3/4	*City of Truro*
Exeter	57 3/4	*City of Gloucester*
Tiverton Junc	72 1/4	*City of Truro*
Whiteball	76 3/4	*City of Exeter*
Wellington	79 1/2	*City of Truro*
Bedminster	119	*City of Exeter*
Pylle Hill	120	*City of Truro*

*Including *Speed Records on British Railways*.

So far as journal times are concerned *City of Gloucester* tied with *City of Truro* to Newton Abbot; between Exeter St David's and Tiverton Junction it was only that it was passing Exeter and not stopping that gave it a slight advantage over *City of Exeter*. Nevertheless *City of Truro* made by 4½ minutes the fastest actual overall time from Plymouth Millbay to Pylle Hill, though its fame and ultimate preservation as a national relic could be regarded as representing as much a collective honour to the achievements of the class as a whole in the Ocean Mail contest as on its individual attainments. The locomotive was the first British, and almost certainly the first in the world, to 'do the ton'.

The Engineer fitly rounded-off contemporary comment on this great run and the magnificent continuation to Paddington with the 7ft 8in 4-2-2 No 3065 *Duke of Connaught* by reminding its readers, editorially, that the men on that train had travelled faster than any men on earth at that time; the engineering press had to wait several years before Rous-Marten saw fit to reveal publicly the maximum speed he had

One of the Atbaras rebuilt with the Standard No 4 boiler, No 3403 *Hobart*. (W. J. Reynolds)

clocked in the descent of the Wellington bank, and the lustre of the performance as a whole was well established before that revelation. There is only one question to be asked finally: whether any better time from Bristol to Paddington would have been made if the fresh engine had been another City, and not a 7ft 8in single. The Cities had shown in 1903 and in the running of the Ocean Mails that they could continue indefinitely at 75 to 77mph on level track with loads of this magnitude. On the very slight falling gradient between Shrivenham and Westbourne Park *Duke of Connaught* averaged exactly 80mph, with a maximum of 84mph near Taplow, and on this comparison alone it is doubtful whether a City would have made better time. The only thing is that time might have been saved west of Swindon by more rapid accelerations from the various slacks, and faster ascents of the Box Tunnel and Dauntsey banks. The final question with the benefit of hindsight is to ask how the performance might have differed with the engine in its later state, super-heated and with piston valves. The running of the Ocean Mails in 1904 was a triumphant demonstration of what the original valve design and exhaust arrangements could do.

CHAPTER SEVEN

LATER DOUBLE-FRAMED 4-4-0s AND THE REBUILDS

The last batch of Camel class 4-4-0s with parallel domeless boiler, Nos 3425-3432, came out in May 1903, and their numbers immediately preceded in chronological order those of the Cities. Then there was a pause of four months, and in September a new standard boiler made its appearance. This was the first version of the taper-barrel Standard No 2, and was fitted to the first of a new batch of Camels, No 3443 *Birkenhead*. It will be noted that the number followed that of the last of the Cities. The new boiler was not primarily intended for the Camels. Churchward's celebrated drawing of January 1901 showing his six proposed standard classes included only two sizes of boiler: a 15ft 0in barrel with a 9ft 0in firebox for the ten-wheeled locomotives, and a smaller one with an 11ft 2in barrel and an 8ft 0in firebox for the 2-6-2 tank, the 4-4-2 tank, and the 4-4-0 express passenger. Both boilers were originally planned with a 5ft 0in diameter barrel, so as to permit of maximum interchangeability of details, and tooling. However, weight restrictions made it necessary to develop a lighter edition of his

proposed boiler with the 8ft 0in firebox. This had, in any case, been shortened to 7ft 0in for the Standard No 4, but the lighter version, which did not permit of the use of the same flanging plates as the big No 1, became known as the Standard No 2, and was designed primarily for the prototype 2-6-2 tank No 99, which was completed at Swindon in September 1903.

Be that as it may, Churchward had in commission at that time thirty-nine Atbaras and sixty Camels with the parallel version of the No 2 boiler, and the advantage of having a taper-barrel version interchangeable with the older one was no doubt irresistible. Like the rebuilding of the Atbara class locomotive *Mauritius* with the prototype No 4 taper boiler it was another step towards the integration of the main standardisation programme with the equipment of the older inside-cylinder locomotives. The firebox of the taper-barrel Standard

A Camel, No 3455 *Australia,* one of the earliest to be built new (January 1904) with half-cone taper boiler. *(P. H. Counsell)*

No 2 was 7ft 0in long, 4ft 0in wide at the bottom, 5ft 3in wide at the upper portion of the throat plate and 4ft 9in wide at the back plate. The grate sloped downwards 1ft 0in, and the width of the waterways at the foundation rings was uniformly 3½in, a dimension that was carried generally through the entire range of Great Western standard boilers. The barrel of the Standard No 2 was 11ft 0in long as originally planned, but the rear barrel plate tapered over a length of 5ft 6in from 5ft 0½in at the throat plate to 4ft 5⅛in at the front. Such were the elements of what was sometimes called the 'half-cone' boiler, to distinguish it from the later No 2 in which the tapering extended for three-quarters of the length of the barrel. The Standard No 4 used on the Cities had the same length of firebox as the No 2 but was larger in the barrel.

As compared to the domeless parallel boilers used on the first Camels, which had 277 tubes of 1⅞in diameter, a tube heating surface of 1538sq ft, and a grate area of 21.45sq ft, the half-cone Standard No 2 had 289 tubes of 1⅝in diameter, a tube heating surface of 1396.58sq ft and a grate area of 20.35sq ft. As on the No 4 boilers fitted to the Cities the boiler pressure was raised to 195lb/sq in. The short-cone No 2 boiler was fitted to thirty 5ft 8in 4-4-0s built between September 1903 and April 1904. The class, which by the latter date mustered ninety-one locomotives, was still known variously as Camels, or sometimes as Avalons.

The 1903-4 batch built new with short-cone No 2 taper boilers were:

3443	Birkenhead	3458	Natal Colony
3444	Cardiff	3459	Toronto
3445	Ilfracombe	3460	Montreal
3446	Swindon	3461	Ottawa
3447	Newport	3462	Winnipeg
3448	Paddington	3463	Vancouver
3449	Reading	3464	Jamaica
3450	Swansea	3465	Trinidad
3451	Taunton	3466	Barbados
3452	Wolverhampton	3467	Empire of India
3453	Dominion of	3468	Calcutta
	Canada	3469	Madras
3454	New Zealand	3470	Bombay
3455	Australia	3471	Queensland
3456	Albany	3472	Columbia
3457	Tasmania		

One must admit that the names of the first ten were not very imaginative, and one can heartily sympathise with the Traffic Department in asking for them to be removed. For the first month of its existence No 3446 was named *Liverpool*, but where the later name was concerned there were apparently none of the old doubts raised when the last of the Castles, No 7037, was named *Swindon*, with felicitous ceremony, on 15 November 1950 by Her Majesty Queen Elizabeth II, when Princess Elizabeth.

In 1906 a further batch of thirty 5ft 8in 4-4-0s was completed at Swindon, having the long, or three-quarter coned boiler, and by that time it was evident that the inspiration for naming was drying up, because the whole batch was originally put into traffic unnamed. Their

One of the first 5ft 8in 4-4-0s to have the three-quarter cone taper boiler. Unnamed when built in May 1906, later *George A. Wills. (P. J. T. Reed)*

1.10pm Bristol-Penzance express passing Dawlish Warren. No 3357 *Smeaton*, then fitted with ¾-cone taper boiler. *(R. J. Purves)*

numbers were 3701 to 3730. The personal names added later, as under, were mostly those of directors:

3701 *Stanley Baldwin*
3702 *John G. Griffiths*
3703 *James Mason*
3704 *A. H. Mills*
3705 *George A. Wills*
3706 *John W. Wilson*
3707 *Francis Mildmay*
3708 *Sir Arthur Yorke*
3720 *Inchcape*
3724 *Joseph Shaw*

Sir Arthur Yorke was Chief Inspecting Officer of Railways, of the Board of Trade. Two others came in for topographical names, 3712 *Aberystwyth* and 3729 *Weston-super-Mare*, to be duly removed later, but the rest of this batch ran nameless throughout their existence.

While the construction of this group of locomotives was in progress the prototype, No 3312 *Bulldog*, originally classified as a variant of the Duke class, was rebuilt in March 1906 with a three-quarter coned Standard No 2 boiler, and from that time onwards the domeless boilered 5ft 8in 4-4-0s became known as the Bulldog class. This was a natural replacement of a one-off prototype boiler, but when it was followed between October 1906 and January 1909 by the rebuilding of eighteen more Dukes with three-quarter coned No 2 boilers, it seemed that a plan was afoot to convert the entire Duke class to tapered boilers. This, however, did not happen. In addition to the eighteen to be listed

later, and *Bulldog* itself, there was another Duke that had acquired a domeless boiler of the parallel Camel type in February 1903. This was No 3273 *Armorel*, which must surely have held the Swindon record for changes, not merely of individual boiler, but of boiler types. Although it is carrying this particular story a little ahead of our period, these changes make diverting reading:

No 3273 *Armorel* (later No 3306)

Date	Boiler
November 1896	Built new: domed, flush round-topped
February 1902	Parallel domeless
April 1906	Half-coned Standard No 2
October 1910	Three-quarter coned No 2
June 1912	Half-coned No 2 superheated
September 1914	Three-quarter coned No 2 superheated
June 1933	Standard No 3
January 1939	Scrapped

Armorel, by the acquisition of a domeless boiler in 1902, was the first of the Dukes to join the Camel or Avalon class, but passing through the intermediate stage of a half-coned taper boiler from 1906 was not fully assimilated to the rest of the ex-Duke conversions until 1910, and by that time two of the others had gone back one step, to half-coned boilers. The eighteen Dukes that were converted to Bulldogs, with their dates of conversion are set out on the next page.

3253	*Pendennis Castle*	February 1908
3262	*Powderham*	October 1906
3263	*Sir Lancelot*	December 1907
3264	*St. Anthony*	July 1907
3268	*River Tamar*	June 1907
3269	*Tintagel*	May 1907
3279	*Exmoor*	December 1907
3280	*Falmouth*	January 1909
3282	*Maristowe*	July 1907
3286	*St. Just*	September 1908
3316	*Isle of Guernsey*	February 1908
3318	*Jupiter*	February 1908
3322	*Mersey*	November 1907
3324	*Quantock*	December 1908
3325	*St. Columb*	December 1908
3327	*Somerset*	May 1908
3330	*Vulcan*	December 1908
3331	*Weymouth*	July 1907

Thus by January 1909 including *Armorel* and *Bulldog* itself, the class was 141 strong, the most numerous of all Great Western passenger engines until the days of the Collett standard classes. There were three types of domeless boilers, and these began to be interchanged among a number of classes besides the Bulldogs. The Dean 7ft 8in 4-2-2 singles got some of the parallel type, with the high raised Belpaire firebox. Some of the Dukes also acquired them, while one of the Armstrongs, No 16 *Brunel*, and five of the Badmintons—*Barrington, Alexander Hubbard, Monarch, Charles Mortimer* and *Samson* had spells with these boilers before eventually getting the long-coned Standard No 2. There was no significance in these changes. It was just a case of putting the first available No 2 boiler on to an engine in the Works for heavy repair. The change that *was* significant was that applied to the Badmintons. In 1905-6 it was intended to incorporate them in the City class, and all except three received Standard No 4 boilers; later, when the time came for superheating, they were fitted with long-coned Standard No 2 boilers. So far as non-superheater engines were concerned, Churchward had reached finality in the No 4 boiler put onto the Cities in 1903, and in the long-coned No 2 used on the Bulldogs from April 1904 onwards. The cylinders, valves and valve gear remained standard throughout the entire range.

An activity that might have seemed no more than incidental, and concerned more with the maintenance of individual engines than anything else, was the amount of frame strengthening that became necessary from 1904 onwards. The

reason for it might seem rather obscure. The inner and outer plates on the double-framed engines from the Dukes onward were ¾in thick, and one would imagine that the combined strength of two such plates on each side of the engine would provide a more robust framing than the single 1⅛in plates of the new standard engines. But it was desirable to tie each pair of inner and outer together as close as possible to the coupled wheel axle boxes, otherwise the ¾in plates would tend to flex under the loads carried in the frames. The axles themselves had generous bearings: 8in long in the outside frame and 7in in the inside. With the introduction of more powerful double-framed engines, and particularly those with 6ft 8½in driving wheels the cross-ties between inner and outer frames could not be placed near enough to the axle-boxes to counteract flexing, which eventually caused frame cracking. So one saw the rather extraordinary expedient of patching on the frames. Naturally the patches were put on inside, but their presence could be detected by the array of rivets showing on the outer surface of the frames. As the frames got older and more susceptible to cracking more and more patching was added.

One of the greatest unsolved queries on Great Western locomotive practice of the period is why Churchward continued the use of double frames on the inside-cylinder 4-4-0 engines, after Dean had definitely retired. It was not just a case of completing orders already on the shops. From midsummer of 1902 he built 125 more 4-4-0s with double frames, continuing until January 1910. The design certainly had some advantages. It made possible a total length of bearing of 15in on each side of the engine. Then the short length of inside bearing enabled the big-end journal to be made 5in wide, with massive crank webs 4½in wide. The cylinders could be spaced farther apart leaving more room for the steam chest, and greater space for the exhaust passages from the valves to the blastpipe. On the other hand, it made for heavier construction, and higher first cost. The outside-cylinder Counties, which feature in the second volume, were exactly the same weight as the Cities, although having a nominal tractive effort some 15 per cent greater. Another disadvantage of the double-framed engines was the much higher incidence of broken crank axles. The highest concentration of weight on the axle was outside the wheels, and this accentuated flange blows at the rail. A careful record at Swindon indicated that failure of crank axles, either by complete

Flower class No 4102 *Begonia* showing deeper and strengthened frames. *(British Railways)*

fracture, or through hairline cracks indicating fatigue flaws, were roughly three times as many on double-, as on single-framed engines—which merely heightens the mystery as to why Churchward kept building the type for so long.

The picturesquely named Flower series of 6ft 8½in 4-4-0s of 1908 was a case in point. By that time Churchward had thirty of the new outside-cylinder Counties at work, part of the main standardisation plan. The Flowers had deeper frames than the Atbaras, and consequently were heavier; in fact their adhesion weight was 35 tons 14 cwt, compared to 34 tons 6 cwt on the Counties. The weight on the bogie of the latter engines was heavier. Although the Flowers carried the long-cone Standard No 2 boiler and the usual inside cylinder arrangement of valves and valve gear, a certain amount of additional design work had obviously been put into these engines. That they were great favourites of Churchward himself was well known. He was an expert horticulturalist, and it was generally understood that the names of these twenty came from some of the most cherished flowers in his own garden, thus:

4101	*Auricula*	4111	*Anemone*
4102	*Begonia*	4112	*Carnation*
4103	*Calceolaria*	4113	*Hyacinthe*
4104	*Calendula*	4114	*Marguerite*
4105	*Camellia*	4115	*Marigold*
4106	*Campanula*	4116	*Mignonette*
4107	*Cineraria*	4117	*Narcissus*
4108	*Gardenia*	4118	*Polyanthus*
4109	*Lobelia*	4119	*Primrose*
4110	*Petunia*	4120	*Stephanotis*

When new, a number of the Flower class went to South Wales. Although 4-6-0 locomotives worked as far as Cardiff they did not then often

No 4120 *Stephanotis*, decorated in honour of the King of Sweden. *(British Railways)*

No 4118 *Polyanthus* hauling a very heavy down Worcester express passing Old Oak Common. *(L & GRP)*

go beyond, so when the GWR began to work up the Ocean Mail traffic via Fishguard, tempting the inward-bound Cunard liners to set down passengers and mails by tender and save a day on the journey from New York to London, compared to going via Liverpool and the LNWR, the new 4-4-0s were put on to the job. Truth to tell, 4-4-0s were not ideal for the sharp gradients of the main line west of Cardiff, particularly around Swansea and west of Carmarthen, and a good deal of assisting engine mileage was necessary. That unsuitable engines were sometimes provided for this latter duty was sadly revealed on 3 October 1904, in a bad accident to the up New Milford boat train at Loughor Bridge east of Llanelly. The train was a very heavy one, worked by one of the latest of the Camel class, No 3460 *Montreal*; to assist in the steep climb up to Cockett Tunnel a 0-6-0 outside-framed saddle tank had been put on as pilot at Llanelly. They were going hard to take a run at the 2½ miles of 1 in 50-53 when the speed became too much for the leading engine, which began rolling so violently as to overturn. *Montreal* remained on the line, but the sudden stop caused general destruction in rear, and the casualty list was long.

The introduction of the Flowers came at a time when the gradual move towards standardisation of the boilers of all the inside-cylinder 4-4-0s was beginning, and which eventually led to all except the unrebuilt Dukes and the twenty Cities having the long-cone Standard No 2 boiler. Whether or not it was

Churchward's own suggestion we do not know but all the 6ft 8½in locomotives with the No 2 boiler became classified as Flowers, whatever their several origins. As thus constituted the class eventually comprised:

		New Number from 1912
20	Badmintons	4100-4119
29	Atbaras	4120-4148
20	Flowers	4149-4168
4	Armstrongs	4169-4172

The Armstrongs did not become strictly part of the Flower class until they were rebuilt with 6ft 8½in coupled wheels, at various dates between 1915 and 1923. In mentioning the 1912 renumbering I have drawn ahead somewhat of my present period, to a time when the modernisation programme also included super-heating.

Although by the time the Flowers were built Churchward had abandoned the more fanciful features of Great Western locomotive livery, substituting black underframes for the previous crimson, and using a simpler form of lining out on boilers, cab sides and tenders, the Flowers were always magnificently turned out. As if to compensate for the loss of other finery they were fitted with large diameter copper-capped chimneys, though this did not signify any change in design. The large chimney was purely ornamental; the 'innards' remained the same. It was at this time that the lettering on the tenders was changed. The closely intertwined scroll letters *GWR* which dated from the Dean era were the nearest that Swindon got to emulating the practice of Crewe in making as inconspicous as possible the ownership of its engines. It was in keeping with the new-found expansionist attitude of the company that *GREAT WESTERN* should be proudly displayed on its tenders. The inclusion of the splendid gartered crest put on the finishing touch. But alas, like many of the 'heraldic' devices sported by the railways of Great Britain and Ireland, and some of India too, the Great Western crest, as displayed on locomotives and carriages had no heraldic justification, though this was not pointed out until more than twenty years later. It was after Royal permission had been sought to name No 6000 *King George V* that someone other than railway folk and friendly travellers had Collett's attention drawn to that crest. It was not the heraldic device itself that offended, because it comprised the long-established crests of the cities of London and Bristol; it was the encompassing of them with a garter that was incorrect heraldically, and thereafter the garter was discreetly removed.

There was another important detailed change on the Flowers. Not only were the frames made deeper than on the Atbaras. and reinforced at the back, as can be seen from the riveting on the official photograph of *Begonia*, but there was a change in the bogie. Compounding apart, Churchward had been very impressed with certain details of the de Glehn Atlantics imported from France, and one of these was the bogie. This was adapted with some ingenuity to the outside-framed type used on the inside-cylinder 4-4-0s. Instead of the Dean suspension arrangement, brackets were fixed to the main frames, incorporating an inverted hemisphere. These rested in suitably shaped cups with a flat base, beneath which slid brackets, with a flat top, which were fixed to the bogie frame. The

side control, by a pair of helical springs, was modified from the Dean arrangement to agree with French practice. This modified bogie arrangement, which could be recognised by the absence of the large caps and nuts beneath the bogie frame, was later applied to all the inside-cylinder 4-4-0s, and to the range of standard outside-cylinder locomotives with the bar-frame type of bogie. William Stanier also took it with him to the LMS.

Another change on the Flowers was a reversion to ordinary screw reversing gear. As locomotives became larger, and the reversing mechanism tended to get heavier, there was a general feeling that something ought to be done to lessen the physical labour needed in actuating the gear, and various forms of steam reverser were introduced, notably by Dugald Drummond and James Stirling. From my own footplate experience I have noted that these were fiddling things to adjust and that it was not always easy to get the exact setting of the reverser that was required. Churchward and the Swindon drawing office produced a manually-operated screw reverse that was both easy to adjust and precise in its setting, and this proved another welcome feature in the equipment of the Flowers. Another change was the use of vacuum brake instead of steam brake on the locomotive, though this did not go to the extent of putting brakes on the bogie wheels, as on the standard 4-6-0 express locomotives. From the start the Flowers had the larger 3500-gallon tenders with a raised fender instead of the coal rails on the older type.

The last group of double-framed inside

The Bird series of Bulldogs: No 3733 *Chaffinch* in photographic grey. *(British Railways)*

First call of the *Mauretania* at Fishguard: Nos 4116 *Mignonette* and 4111 *Anemone* wait outside with the second passenger special. *(British Railways)*

3739	*Nightingale*	3743	*Seagull*
3740	*Peacock*	3744	*Skylark*
3741	*Pelican*	3745	*Starling*
3742	*Penguin*		

cylinder 4-4-0s came in 1909-10, with a further series of improved Bulldogs having the modified bogie, deeper frames, and screw reverse. They came in two distinct batches—Nos 3731-5 in May 1909, and Nos 3736-3745 in November 1909 to January 1910. All were named after birds, and one might imagine that Churchward was supplementing his love of gardening with names of his feathered friends, except that one or two of the titles were hardly of garden visitors. The fifteen were:

3731	*Blackbird*	3735	*Flamingo*
3732	*Bullfinch*	3736	*Goldfinch*
3733	*Chaffinch*	3737	*Jackdaw*
3734	*Cormorant*	3738	*Kingfisher*

These were among the last of the GWR 4-4-0s to survive, and all of them came into national ownership in 1948. So far as individual names were concerned, it has always intrigued me to note the locomotives of a class that were chosen for painting in photographic grey for the official photograph. There is every suggestion that Churchward himself made the choices. Among the 4-6-0s, for example, there was *Butleigh Court*, the home of one of his closest personal friends, rather than the first of the Court series, while the chosen engines of the Flower and Bird classes were *Begonia* and *Chaffinch*, probably garden favourites.

CHAPTER EIGHT

HIGH NOON—VINTAGE PERFORMANCE

The six years from the time of the Ocean Mail records to the beginning of 1910 can be regarded as the high noon of the inside-cylinder 4-4-0 on the Great Western Railway. They were used for the inauguration of the Cornish Riviera Express, at first minus the word 'Cornish'; they had the entire main line service in Cornwall to themselves and, except for very occasional incursions by the larger engines, the line west of Cardiff. The 4-2-2 singles still took some trains on the Worcester line but the Atbaras and Cities were moving in, while on the Weymouth line the power was mostly provided by Bulldogs. A

record of the day's working at Paddington on Saturday, 2 July 1904, gave the following examples of 4-4-0 allocation at that time.

It is interesting to note some return workings. *Waterford* had been to Exeter and back in the day, while *Dunedin* had been to Cardiff and back. Although this is primarily a record of 4-4-0 working I put in the up Riviera Express, on which *La France* seems to have had a high-speed spree. The 20-minute late arrival of

Duke class 4-4-0 No 3326 *St. Austell* on train for Penzance, at St Germans. *(W. J. Reynolds)*

DOWN TRAINS from Paddington:

Booked departure time	Destination	No	Locomotive Name
am			
9.00	Torquay	3310	*Waterford*
9.35	Southampton and Weymouth	3333	*Brasenose*
9.45	Reading (local)	3427	*Sir Watkin Wynn*
9.50	Birkenhead	3404	*Lyttleton*
10.10	Riviera Express	3433	*City of Bath*
10.45	Torquay	3397	*Cape Town*
11.20	South Wales (first stop Newport)	3399	*Dunedin*
11.40	Cardiff (semi-fast)	3424	*Sir N. Kingscote*
12.35	Weymouth	3363	*One and All*
pm			
2.00	Oxford via High Wycombe	3417	*C. G. Mott*
2.40	Weymouth	3466	*Barbados*
3.03	Bristol and Ilfracombe	3392	*White*
3.35	South Wales	3383	*Kekewich*
4.25	South of Ireland (Boat train 1st part)	3381	*Maine*
4.30	South of Ireland (Boat train 2nd part)	3411	*St. Johns*
6.10	South Wales	3384	*Omdurman*

UP TRAINS arriving Paddington:

Booked arrival	From	No	Locomotive Name	Actual time
am				
9.32	Swindon	3424	*Sir N. Kingscote*	8½ L
9.55	Waterford (Boat express)	3383	*Kekewich*	15 L
10.10	Didcot	3417	*C. G. Mott*	4½ L
10.55	Swindon (milk train)	3363	*One and All*	RT
11.25	Bristol	3392	*White*	7½ L
pm				
1.00	South Wales	3411	*St. Johns*	5½ L
1.10	Cork Boat Express	3381	*Maine*	2 L
2.00	Bristol (Two-hour train)	3395	*Aden*	7 L
2.47	Bristol (via Devizes)	3425	*Sir W. H. Wills*	1½ E
3.35	Falmouth (non-stop from Exeter)	3376	*Herschell*	RT
4.20	South Wales	3386	*Pembroke*	½ E
5.00	Up Riviera Express	102	*La France*	9 E
6.10	South Wales	3399	*Dunedin*	20 L
6.15	Ilfracombe	3310	*Waterford*	5 E
7.00	Newquay (non-stop from Exeter)	3441	*City of Winchester*	1½ E

Dunedin was mainly due to poor operating. The late A. V. Goodyear, to whose notes I am indebted for these details, said that the 6.15pm Ilfracombe train had got ahead of the South Wales, and the latter when it did approach Paddington, very near to its scheduled time, had to wait a long time outside until a platform was free. One noticeable point is the comparative absence of the Cities, only two out of the ten having been recorded all day. At the time the 4-2-2 singles were still taking an important part in main line express working and no fewer than twenty-six of them were noted during the day, as against eleven Atbaras, two Cities, seven Camels, and the rebuilt Badminton No 3310 *Waterford*, which at that time had a City type boiler.

Coming now to some details of actual

running, much interest was created in the summer of 1903 by the acceleration of some of the best trains between Paddington and Bristol, with the first part of the up 'Dutchman' running non-stop via Badminton, newly opened to passenger traffic on 1 July 1903, in the level two hours. Prior to the introduction of the Riviera Express in the following summer the 10.45am from Paddington ran to Bristol in 2 hours 5 minutes, slipping a coach at Bath. From October of 1903 the departure time was made 10.50am, but all arrival times from Bath westward were the same. These trains were much heavier than those conveyed on the Royal record run, and on the Ocean Mails, and

GWR : 10.45am PADDINGTON-BATH
No 3433 *City of Bath*
Load: 230 tons

Distance Miles		Schedule minutes	Actual min sec	Average speed mph
0.0	Paddington	0	0 00	—
9.1	Southall	12	11 47	47.0
18.5	Slough	21 1/2	20 42	63.3
24.2	Maidenhead	27 1/2	26 00	64.7
31.0	Twyford	34	32 25	63.8
36.0	Reading	39	37 02	65.2
53.1	Didcot	56 1/2	52 37	65.3
60.5	*Milepost 60 1/2*	—	60 00	60.1
77.3	Swindon	81	77 00	59.3
94.0	Chippenham	98	92 31	64.7
101.9	Box	—	100 23	60.2
106.9	Bath	112	105 11*	62.5

* Passing time of main train, at reduced speed

provided an interesting test of City class engine capacity. The first run tabulated, with No 3433 *City of Bath* was made while the schedule was 125 minutes non-stop to Bristol, the Bath slip coach being due to arrive at 12.37pm or in 112 minutes from Paddington, 106.9 miles. It was a good steady run, typical of the constant, uniform performance that became so typical of the City class. The Reverend W. J. Scott who logged the run reported that the train was badly delayed by signals between Bath and Bristol, and eventually arrived late.

On the up road via Badminton he logged an excellent run on the accelerated 12 noon up, though with an Ocean Mail size of load only 150 tons. The principal interest of the run, however, arose from the train being subjected to heavy slacks on the new line, because there were places where the embankments had not fully consolidated, and had been disturbed by heavy rain. Scott was lucky in that the train got a clear road after rejoining the old line at Wootton Bassett. I have tabulated three other runs on this same train, logged by the Reverend W. A. Dunn, which are more creditable to the locomotive department than to the operating. The notebooks compiled by this very careful recorder show run after run on the most sharply-timed

The first 4-4-0 locomotive to have the taper boiler, No 3405 *Mauritius* on up Bristol express. *(Locomotive Publishing Co)*

GWR 12 NOON BRISTOL-PADDINGTON

Run No:		1	2	3	4
Locomotive No:		3435	3435	3382	3737
Locomotive Name:		City of Bristol	City of Bristol	Mafeking	City of Gloucester
Load, tons		165	150	175	150

Distance Miles		Schedule minutes	Actual min sec	Actual min sec	Actual min sec	Actual min sec
0.0	BRISTOL (Temple Meads)	0	0 00	0 00	0 00	0 00
2.0	Milepost 2		4 38	4 47	4 37	—
4.0	Milepost 4		7 53	7 30	7 50	—
4.8	Filton Junc	7	8 39	8 16	9 05	8 52
—			pws	pws	pws	pws
17.6	Badminton		24 46	24 06	28 03	24 40
27.6	Milepost 90		33 27	33 15	36 56	—
—			pws	pws	—	pws
34.7	Wootton Bassett	36	43 41	43 18	40 43	42 40
40.3	SWINDON	42	50 01	48 58	45 23	47 19
—			signals	—	pws	—
51.1	Uffington		62 11	58 32	57 26	56 29
—			—	—	signals	—
64.5	Didcot	66	76 09	70 16	69 50	67 55
76.0	Pangbourne		86 01	81 03	83 35	—
—			signals	signals	—	—
81.6	READING	83	93 16	86 48	86 29	82 55
86.6	Twyford		98 49	91 53	—	87 32
93.4	Maidenhead	95	104 39	97 33	98 33	93 10
—			—	signals	—	—
99.1	SLOUGH	101	109 18	102 43	104 07	97 53
108.5	Southall	109	117 29	111 52	111 30	105 18
—			signals	—	pws	—
117.6	PADDINGTON	120	129 01	121 53	125 13	115 18
Net times minutes:			109 1/2	115	118	110

express trains, badly delayed by signals, chiefly through slower trains running behind time being given priority at junctions, and in certain cases being allowed to continue on the main line, causing continual delay. For the most part, the drivers of the crack expresses were doing their best, regaining time whenever possible. One can only think that it needed superhuman efforts and wholesale checking of trains to left and right to keep the line so clear for the Ocean Mails.

On the first of the four Bristol two-hour runs, one could understand the eight minutes lost to Swindon by engineering restrictions on the Badminton line, but then it was not until after Wantage Road that the driver began to get really clear signals. Didcot was passed at 73mph and speed lay between 69 and 73mph onwards to Goring troughs. Then the train was practically stopped by signals in the approach to Reading. There was a grand recovery, with an average of 70.8mph between mileposts 29 and 5, including a long sustained 75mph around Slough, but there was another check outside Paddington. The net time was no more than 109½ minutes, an average of 64.3mph. On the second run the same engine and driver, Kirby, got a better road from Swindon and ran at 68 to 72mph continuously from Shrivenham to Didcot. The

check at Reading was less severe, down only to 25mph, and with a good recovery to a sustained 73mph from Maidenhead onwards there was a good chance of getting in on time, had it not been for yet another signal check, at Slough that time.

The third run, with Atbara No 3382 *Mafeking*, which came to a violent end in the Henley-in-Arden smash of 1911, began in promising style with an unhindered spin downhill from Badminton, and a sustained maximum of 75mph near Little Somerford. But the permanent way check just after Swindon, and a signal check at Didcot, seemed to take all the heart out of the running. The final check, at West London Junction was very slight, and cost no more than forty seconds. In contrast, the last run, with *City of Gloucester*, must have been exhilarating to record. After passing Swindon 5¼ minutes late the train got a clear road and 57.4 miles from Uffington to Southall took no more than 49 minutes 21 seconds, an average of 69.8mph. With loads of these modest tonnages it must be admitted that even the two-hour schedule was very easy for such fast and capable locomotives as the Atbaras and Cities. Before leaving the Bristol trains I may mention three other runs with Atbaras, with heavier loads, on which Bath was reached, non-stop from Paddington in 117¼ minutes with 190 tons, 119¼ minutes with 215 tons, and 114 minutes with 230 tons, the respective net times being 116, 115 and 110 minutes.

Next we pass on to the Exeter non-stops, and the first of these, made in 1902 when the schedule was 217 minutes, is interesting in that the locomotive was reported as being in a somewhat run-down condition, and uncomfortable to ride. The train left Paddington three minutes late, and in the early stages the driver was not pressing the engine. Speed had not exceeded 63mph to Reading, and then there came a shocking series of checks, which caused an estimated loss of eight minutes. A clear road was not obtained until Wootton Bassett, and then the shaky rattling *Aden* was taken down Dauntsey bank at 82mph, and a sustained 72mph from Box to the very outskirts of Bath. The locomotive was going well again after the long slow through the Bristol area, reaching 71mph at Yatton, but the ensuing checks from another train ahead were crippling, and ultimately a dead stop came outside Taunton. From this driver and engine did well up to Whiteball, attaining 48mph on the rising gradients to Wellington, then falling gradually to 29mph at the tunnel entrance, and 27mph at the summit. A fast run down to Exeter with a twice-repeated maximum of 75mph brought the train into St. David's barely five minutes outside schedule time, while the net time of 203 minutes showed an average speed of 57.4mph.

The companion run with *City of Gloucester*, made in that exciting spring of 1904, was on the revised schedule of 210 minutes after the Paddington departure time was 3.00pm. A clear road was obtained from Ealing to Swindon, and by that time the train was nearly four minutes early, and running inside 'even time'—not difficult with a load of only 150 tons. The maximum on Dauntsey bank was 78mph, and despite a slight check through Box Tunnel, Bath was passed 5¾ minutes early, in a net time of 100½ minutes from Paddington. There was a slight check at Highbridge, but Taunton was passed in great style at 68mph, all but six minutes early. Alas, however, for any hopes of a real 'run' at the Wellington bank! A slow train had been allowed to go ahead, and the six miles between mileposts 164 and 170 took exactly twelve minutes. Whatever it was seems to have been shunted at Wellington, because *City of Gloucester* was able to recover from 20mph through Wellington station to a sustained

GWR : PADDINGTON-EXETER					
Load: tons gross		160		150	
Locomotive No:		3395		3437	
Locomotive Name:		Aden		City of Gloucester	
		Actual		Actual	
Distance Miles		min	sec	min	sec
0.0	PADDINGTON	0	00	0	00
—			—	signals	
9.1	Southall	14	03	13	35
18.5	Slough	23	50	22	51
21.0	Burnham Beeches	26	20	25	02
24.2	Maidenhead	29	26	27	52
31.0	Twyford	36	19	33	45
36.0	READING	41	09	38	06
41.5	Pangbourne	45	26	42	55
—		signals			
48.5	Cholsey	53	11	49	15
53.1	DIDCOT	57	39	53	24
60.0	Milepost 60	signals		60	03
66.5	Uffington	signals		66	15
75.0	Milepost 75	signals		73	57
—			—	signals	
77.3	SWINDON	90	51	77	13
82.9	Wootton Bassett	97	51	83	40
87.7	Dauntsey	102	11	87	58
94.0	CHIPPENHAM	107	25	93	12
98.3	Corsham	111	32	97	30
—			—	pws	
106.9	BATH	119	23	106	23
118.7	Pylle Hill Junc	134	30	120	45
130.0	Yatton	147	18	133	53
—		signals		signals	
151.3	BRIDGWATER	171	21	156	37
—		signals/stop		—	
162.8	TAUNTON	187	01	168	08
165.7	Milepost 166	190	57	signals	
169.7	Milepost 170	196	06	181	56
172.7	Milepost 173	200	47	188	05
173.7	Whiteball Box	202	59	189	54
178.7	Tiverton Junc	208	11	194	35
185.7	Milepost 186	214	01	199	57
191.7	Milepost 192	218	58	204	47
—			—	signals	
193.6	EXETER	221	54	210	33
Schedule time: minutes		217		210	
Net time: minutes		203		188	

31mph on the 1 in 80, and further to 35mph at Whiteball summit. Then the driver let his engine go, and the fifteen miles between posts 177 and 192 were covered at an average speed of 76.3mph, with a maximum of 83mph. Having passed milepost 192 in 204 minutes 47 seconds Exeter had to delay the approach with adverse signals, so that the last 1.6 miles took nearly six minutes! The net time from Paddington on this fine run was no more than 188 minutes, or 62mph overall.

This last run was made on 26 April 1904, and on the following day Mr. Dunn returned to London by the 12.07pm up Torquay express, also a non-stop in 3½ hours. The particular interest of this run is that the locomotive was No No 3440 *City of Truro* with the same driver, Moses Clements, by whom railway history was to be made less than a fortnight later. Details of this run, together with those of two others on the same train, are set out in a further table. The first of these, with Atbara No 3395 *Aden* was made in the same week as that of its down run, and in the same run-down condition. The locomotive made rather heavy weather of the Whiteball climb, falling to 24mph, although the load of 250 tons would have been considered a substantial one at that time. Then after a maximum of 78mph down the bank, speed settled down to a steady and almost unvarying 62mph over the long level to the foot of the Flax

GWR : EXETER-PADDINGTON NON-STOP

Run No:		1	2	3
Locomotive No:		3395	3440	3442
Locomotive Name:		*Aden*	*City of Truro*	*City of Exeter*
Load — coaches		10	10	9
tons		250	260	230
Distance Miles		Actual min sec	Actual min sec	Actual min sec
0.0	EXETER	0 00	0 00	0 00
—		—	—	pws
3.9	*Milepost 190*	7 55	7 27	9 33
—				pws
14.9	Tiverton Junc	21 15	21 21	24 59
19.9	*Whiteball Box*	28 03	28 32	32 47
—				pws
23.9	*Milepost 170*	32 15	32 06	38 34
27.9	*Milepost 166*	35 25	35 31	42 32
30.8	TAUNTON	38 01	38 09	45 11
42.3	Bridgwater	48 54	48 56	54 08
55.9	*Uphill Junc*	62 00	64 01	68 23
64.9	*Milepost 129*	70 50	72 37	76 49
72.9	*Milepost 121*	79 37	80 57	84 55
74.9	*Pylle Hill Junc*	82 45	83 23	87 30
86.7	BATH	99 02	99 08	103 58
—		—	—	pws
91.6	*Milepost 102*	105 49	105 14	111 25
99.6	Chippenham	116 30	115 33	121 50
108.6	*Milepost 85*	125 40	125 13	131 00
—		—	pws	pws
116.3	SWINDON	134 54	133 53	140 20
121.6	*Milepost 72*	140 19	—	146 34
—		pws		
138.6	*Milepost 55*	159 31	156 05	161 00
—		—		
140.5	DIDCOT	161 26	158 48	163 55
—		signals		pws
145.6	*Milepost 49*	—	161 15	169 23
153.6	*Milepost 41*	175 12	169 54	177 14
—		—	pws	—
158.6	READING	180 14	175 58	181 50
170.4	Maidenhead	191 37	188 41	192 15
—		signals	—	—
176.1	Slough	198 36	194 00	197 10
184.5	Southall	208 56	203 19	205 55
—		—	—	pws
193.6	PADDINGTON	220 05	214 23	218 47
Net times: minutes		214	209	200 1/2
Speeds: mph				
Cullompton		52	50	51
Whiteball		24	33	28
Wellington bank		78	77	75
Maximum speed Swindon to Ealing		65	70	75

Bourton bank. As far as Pylle Hill, however, no time had been regained.

City of Truro with a load of 260 tons did very similarly up to Whiteball, touched 77mph down the bank, but then did distinctly inferior work onwards to Yatton. The sustained speed on the long level was only 55 to 57mph, although towards the end of it speed was vigorously worked up to 68mph to charge the Flax Bourton bank, so by this energy and a quicker recovery from the Bristol slowing, *City of Truro* had practically overtaken the run-down *Aden* by the time Bath was passed. On the western part of the journey it was *City of Exeter* on the third run that claims most of the honours. After bad checks at first, it ran the 42.1 miles from Taunton to Milepost 121 in 39 minutes 44 seconds, against the 41 minutes 36 seconds of *Aden* and 42 minutes 48 seconds of *City of Truro*. East of Swindon it was again *City of Exeter* that made the running, with a time of only 78½ minutes for the 77.3 miles to Paddington, despite a slow start, passing Swindon at 30mph and two further checks costing between them seven minutes. *City of Exeter* ran at 75mph between Wantage Road and Didcot, and at 70 to 72mph between Maidenhead and Slough. With a load of 230 tons this was well up to Ocean Mail standards. The work of *City of Truro* was less enterprising. The average speed over the twenty miles between mileposts 65 and 45 was 68.3mph with a maximum of 70mph, and after the check to 22mph at Reading the maximum afterwards was 67mph. The net time of 209 minutes was only one minute inside schedule.

Turning from the West of England to South Wales the Reverend W. A. Dunn took details of a very interesting journey on the 4.30pm Waterford boat train, which he joined at Bath, travelling on through to Neyland, then known as New Milford. This train then called only at Stapleton Road, Cardiff, Landore Junction, Carmarthen Junction, and Haverfordwest, omitting Newport, and making connection to and from Swansea at Landore. The load once again was light, only six coaches, totalling 150 tons gross, and it was brought into Bath on time by Atbara No 3410 *Sydney*. This engine continued to Cardiff, but beset by severe signal checks passing through Newport took 60 minutes 3 seconds instead of the scheduled fifty-five minutes to cover the thirty-six miles from Stapleton Road. At Cardiff *Sydney* was exchanged for another Atbara, No 3377 *Kitchener*, which continued through to New

A scene at Whiteball summit: an up express hauled by a City class locomotive is detaching its pilot, a Badminton with No 4 boiler. *(O. S. Nock collection)*

Milford. Details of the run, as far as Haverford-west, are tabulated. As this journey was made in April, and Cardiff was left at 8.16pm—after dark—Mr Dunn could not make his usual meticulous log of the mileposts.

The climb up to Llanharan is steep only in the last mile (1 in 106), and the line is downhill and level onwards to Bridgend, but after the three

GWR : : WATERFORD BOAT EXPRESS
Load: 6 coaches, 150 tons gross
Locomotives, to Cardiff: 3410 *Sydney*
           to New Milford: 3377 *Kitchener*

Distance Miles		Schedule minutes	Actual min sec	
	BRISTOL (Stapleton			
0.0	Road)	0	0 00	
4.3	Patchway		10 34	
7.4	Pilning Junc		14 15	
8.9	*Severn Tunnel East*		16 21	
13.3	*Severn Tunnel West*		22 04	
			signals	
24.2	NEWPORT		40 16	
			signals	
36.0	CARDIFF	55	60 03	
14.0	*Summit* (Llanharan)		19 00	
17.0	Pencoed		22 30	
20.8	Bridgend	27	26 40	
26.2	Pyle	34	33 48	
32.9	Port Talbot (pass)	42	40 15	signal
			41 15	stop
38.5	Neath	50	52 20	
45.0	LANDORE JUNC	60	63 30	
4.8	Gowerton	9	13 03	
6.9	Loughor		15 20	
10.6	LLANELLY (pass)	18	20 00	signal
			24 05	stop
14.5	Pembrey		30 35	
27.6	*Towy Castle Box*		45 22	
	CARMARTHEN			
30.3	JUNC	43	50 02	
8.2	St Clears		12 35	
14.0	Whitland		19 10	
19.4	Clynderwen		26 05	
25.9	Clarbeston Rd		33 35	
31.2	HAVERFORDWEST	42	39 40	

miles up to Stormy Siding, which is not noted in the log, the train must have come pretty smartly down Pyle bank to take only 6 minutes 27 seconds to the signal stop at Port Talbot. This Mr Dunn estimates to have cost about four minutes in running. By smart station working at Landore the train left only 1¾ minutes late, but the uphill start to Cockett, two miles at 1 in 52-71, and the similar descent to Gowerton, was not as vigorous as the timetable expected, and then the operating people at Llanelly obliged with a dead stand for signals, lasting four minutes. There did not seem any great disposition to make up time afterwards, because the 13.1 level miles from Pembrey to Towy Castle box took 14 minutes 47 seconds, and there was a loss of seven minutes on schedule to Carmarthen Junction. This was the old station, long since dismantled. By far the best running was made over the heavily undulating road beyond, with a gain of 2¼ minutes to Haverford-west, but in the absence of maximum and minimum speed there is not much to be added by way of comment to the tabulated details.

It was in the summer of 1907 that the Great Western inaugurated their celebrated day trips from Paddington to Killarney, with a train leaving at 8.40pm and running non-stop over the 261.4 miles to Fishguard Harbour. Rous-Marten was invited to travel on the first occasion, Tuesday, 24 September, but unfortunately he recorded little of the locomotive performance on the less known and more interesting part of the line west of Cardiff. He comments upon the

4-4-0 No 3408, originally *Ophir* renamed *Killarney* for the first 'day excursion', run in 1907. *(British Railways)*

GWR : 8.40pm PADDINGTON-FISHGUARD
Non-stop Excursion Train
4–4–0 No 3408 *Killarney*
Load: 5 coaches, 180 tons full

darkness of the night, but the conditions cannot have been very different from those during the Race to the North in 1895, when he secured such complete records of the Caledonian running in the small hours. To haul the beautiful train of five 70ft coaches, one of the Atbaras rebuilt with the No 4 boiler, No 3408 *Ophir* was used. It was renamed *Killarney* specially for the occasion, and carried the latter name for the rest of its existence. The schedule laid down allowed 5 hours 5 minutes for the non-stop run, and as the accompanying log shows some fast work was needed in the early stages, attaining even time by Goring. This was the first passenger train ever to pass Cardiff without stopping, and Rous-Marten records that the platforms were densely crowded with spectators to see the train go through at 11.00pm. One would dearly like to have had more details of how the ensuing 116.3 miles on to Fishguard were covered in 145 minutes 24 seconds but this, the longest non-stop run ever attempted on the GWR, finished 6½ minutes early. On the return trip,

Distance Miles		Actual min	sec	Average speed mph
0.0	PADDINGTON	0	00	—
5.7	Ealing	8	10	41.9
13.2	West Drayton	15	32	61.1
18.5	Slough	20	19	66.4
24.2	Maidenhead	25	43	63.4
31.0	Twyford	32	03	64.3
36.0	READING	36	18	70.6
44.8	Goring	44	32	64.0
53.1	Didcot	52	14	64.7
77.3	SWINDON	76	16	60.3
82.9	Wootton Bassett	81	49	60.5
100.0	Badminton	99	58	56.5
112.0	*Stoke Gifford West*	113	44	52.4
122.5	*Severn Tunnel Exit*	125	00	55.9
133.4	NEWPORT	138	42	47.8
145.1	CARDIFF	153	01	49.1
—		many slacks		
189.6	Landore	207	29	49.0
200.1	LLANELLY	221	58	43.4
220.2	Carmarthen Bridge Junc	244	30	53.5
261.4	FISHGUARD	298	25	45.9

the guard's journal gave a time of 294½ minutes, an average speed of 53.3mph.

Two years later, on 30 August 1909 came another milestone in Great Western train

| Train | Load | | Locomotives | |
	Coaches	Tons tare	No	Name
Mails only	3	90	3381	*Maine*
1st Passenger	10	274	3402 / 4108	*Halifax* / *Gardenia*
2nd Passenger	10	295	4111 / 4116	*Anemone* / *Mignonette*

running, in which the inside-cylinder 4-4-0s played a notable part. This was an Ocean liner special, or rather three of them, run in connection with the first call at Fishguard of the *Mauretania*, on her east-bound run from New York. From Fishguard the three trains were loaded, and hauled as on opposite page.

All three trains ran non-stop from Fishguard to Cardiff, where locomotives were changed. On the eastern part of the journey the then-new Star class locomotives of the 'King' series were used. For the record these were, respectively, 4023 *King George*, 4021 *King Edward* and 4022 *King William*. Of the 4-4-0s used west of Cardiff, *Maine* was an Atbara, *Halifax* had been rebuilt as a City, and the other three were Flowers, only just over a year old. Rous-Marten had died in the previous year, and the accompanying log of the first passenger special was compiled by G. A. Sekon, the founder editor of *The Railway Magazine*.

The start was excellent, seeing that for two miles out of Fishguard the climbing to Manorowen is up at 1 in 50. Speed was held in on the curving lengths down to Wolf's Castle, not exceeding 61mph, but east of Clarbeston Road Sekon clocked a maximum of 82mph beyond which there was a relaying check at Cardigan Junction. Speed had to be reduced to 10mph over the bascule bridge at Drawbridge Junction. There was some fast running round the level coastal section to Llanelly, but after two more checks the very steep ascent to Cockett brought speed down to 19½mph, after 2¼ miles at 1 in 53-50. In the meantime the train had

GWR : *MAURETANIA* SPECIAL, FISHGUARD-CARDIFF
Locomotives: 3402 *Halifax* (leading) and 4108 *Gardenia*
Load: 10 coaches, 310 tons full

Distance Miles		Schedule minutes	Actual min sec	Average speed mph
0.0	FISHGUARD	0	0 00	—
3.1	*Manorowen Box*		7 50	23.7
15.7	Clarbeston Road	24	21 50	54.0
—			pws	—
27.7	Whitland		32 44	66.1
33.4	St Clears		38 34	58.6
36.8	Sarnau		42 04	58.3
41.2	*Drawbridge Junc*		47 22	49.8
41.6	*Carmarthen Junc*	52	47 57	41.2
48.0	Ferryside		54 46	56.3
52.2	Kidwelly		58 35	66.0
57.4	Pembrey		63 07	68.9
61.3	LLANELLY		66 28	69.8
—			pws	—
65.0	Loughor		69 54	64.5
67.0	Gowerton		72 10	53.2
—			pws	—
69.7	Cockett		76 55	34.1
71.8	Landore	91	slacks	—
74.0	Llansamlet		83 30	39.1
76.3	Skewen		86 25	47.3
78.3	NEATH		89 34	38.2
83.9	PORT TALBOT		95 58	52.5
90.6	Pyle		102 23	62.7
96.0	BRIDGEND	119	109 04	48.4
99.8	Pencoed		113 41	49.3
102.6	Llanharan		116 55	51.7
105.1	Llantrissant		119 31	57.6
109.5	Peterston		123 41	63.5
112.2	St Fagans		126 21	60.7
113.9	Ely		127 51	68.0
116.3	CARDIFF	142	130 58	—

The first *Mauretania* passenger special ready to leave Fishguard, hauled by Nos 3402 *Halifax* and 4108 *Gardenia*; the locomotives of the second special can be seen in the background. *(Locomotive Publishing Co)*

been drawing so well ahead of the working times that those on board began to hope for a 4½-hour run to Paddington instead of the five hours scheduled. Eventually the two engines brought their 310-ton train into Cardiff eleven minutes early by the provisional working times.

From South Wales there are next two fast runs over the North-to-West main line, between Hereford and Shrewsbury, both with Badminton class locomotives, at the time when they were running with City class boilers. On the 12.26pm southbound train No 3311 *Wynnstay* had a light train of only four coaches, 100 tons gross, and ran the 51 miles in exactly 61 minutes, gaining two minutes on schedule. The initial 12.8 mile up to Church Stretton took 21 minutes 20 seconds after which thirty-four miles to Moreton-on-Lugg took 33½ minutes, with speed at no time exceeding 70mph. On the 4.15pm northbound from Hereford, No 3300 *Hotspur* had a seven-coach train of 175 tons all told. A minute was dropped on the sharp initial timing of sixteen minutes for the 12.6 miles to Leominster, but then the 25.6 miles up to Church Stretton were covered in exactly half an hour, and the summit passed three minutes early. With no exceptional downhill speed and a very slow run into Shrewsbury the 51.0 miles were completed in 63 minutes 1 second, arriving five minutes early.

The opening of the new route from Birmingham to Bristol via Stratford-on-Avon and Cheltenham in 1908 gave additional scope for the 4-4-0s to show their paces, though in the

period under review the loads were mostly light. The northbound road from Stratford to Birmingham with the lengthy Henley bank of 7½ miles at 1 in 150, and a concluding 1¾ miles at 1 in 181 to Earlswood Lakes provided a good test of engine capacity. A Flower, No 4109 *Lobelia*, with a load of 130 tons, began the climb at 65mph but did not fall below 50¾mph at the top of the 1 in 150, and with a maximum of 77½mph at Yardley Wood passed Hall Green, 20.1 miles from Stratford, in 22 minutes 55 seconds. Another of the class, No 4114 *Marguerite*, hauling 200 tons began the climb at 54½mph, fell to 46¾mph on its steepest pitch, and attained 70½mph afterwards, passing Hall Green in 25 minutes 5 seconds.

The late A. V. Goodyear gave me details of a fine run he logged with No 3374 *Baden Powell* in 1906, when it was on the Birmingham non-stop from Paddington with a load of no less than thirteen bogies and a six-wheeler, 360 tons all told. The train was slowed to 15mph at Southall, but then the ensuing 77.1 miles to Banbury were covered in 82 minutes 20 seconds pass to stop. Speed reached 60mph soon after Langley, and then the forty-five miles from Slough to Oxford took only 46¼ minutes. On the rising gradients from Oxford splendid work was done with no more than 20¾ minutes taken over the 19.2 miles to King's Sutton. But this heavy work had taken its toll, and a stop for water had to be made at Banbury. The run showed that these moderate-powered engines, then with parallel domeless boiler and only 180lb/sq in pressure, could sustain a speed of around 60mph on level track with a load as great as 360 tons.

A run on this same train, the 2.15pm from Paddington with a 'normal' load of 190 tons is of

Armstrong class 4-4-0 No 16 *Brunel*, with parallel domeless boiler, as running 1901-1909. *(L & GRP)*

unusual interest in that it was hauled by Armstrong No 16 *Brunel*, when running with a parallel domeless boiler, as shown in the photograph on page 92; in running there was nothing exceptional with this moderate load.

When the new route to Birmingham, via Bicester, was opened in 1910, although at first the loads of most of the trains were very light, 4-6-0s were generally used; on those occasions when one of them was not available the inside-cylinder 4-4-0s were used with great success. As will be told in the second volume of this book the outside-cylindered Counties had some regular turns and did very fine work, but here I am concerned with the older locomotives. There is first of all a very fast run from Leamington to Paddington with one of the Badmintons, *Grosvenor*, in the second state, with a Standard No 4 non-superheated boiler. The average speeds are shown in the log, but the recorder, Mr J. C. Keyte, noted the unusual maximum of 77½mph on the new line below Bicester—unusual, that was, for the year 1910, but this was nothing to the descent of the Gerrards Cross bank where the maximum was no less than 88mph. These speeds were in striking contrast to the timorous efforts of *Brunel*.

GWR : LEAMINGTON-PADDINGTON
4—4—0 No 3298 *Grosvenor* (with Standard No 4 boiler)
Load: 190 tons tare; 195 tons full

Distance Miles		Schedule minutes	Actual min sec	Average speeds mph
0.0	LEAMINGTON	0	0 00	—
6.1	Southam Road		9 23	39.0
			pws	—
11.1	Fenny Compton		16 25	42.6
16.2	Cropredy		22 16	52.4
19.8	BANBURY	23 1/2	25 31	66.5
24.9	Aynho Junc	28 1/2	30 04	67.3
30.1	Ardley		35 32	57.2
33.9	Bicester		38 44	71.2
43.2	Ashendon Junc	45	46 35	71.1
47.2	Haddenham		50 34	60.0
52.6	Princes Risboro'	54	55 55	60.5
55.1	Milepost 22		58 47	52.3
60.8	HIGH WYCOMBE	63	64 21	61.5
65.6	Beaconsfield		70 05	50.2
69.9	Gerrards Cross		74 03	64.9
77.0	Northolt Junc	79	79 18	81.2
82.7	Park Royal		83 55	74.3
			signals	—
87.3	PADDINGTON	92	92 19	—

From the late A. V. Goodyear I had details of a superlative run with one of the Cities, No 3406 *Melbourne* on the 12.13pm two-hour express from Birmingham to Paddington. When the new line was first opened, most of the London expresses leaving Birmingham carried portions

GWR 12.13pm BIRMINGHAM-PADDINGTON
4—4—0 No 3406 *Melbourne*
Load: to Leamington: 295 tons
to Paddington: 180 tons

Distance Miles		Actual min sec	Average speeds mph
	BIRMINGHAM (Snow		
0.0	Hill)	0 00	—
3.2	Tyseley	5 26	—
7.0	Solihull	9 47	52.4
17.1	Hatton	19 45	61.0
21.3	Warwick	23 20	70.2
23.3	LEAMINGTON	25 35	—
6.1	Southam Road	9 35	38.2
11.1	Fenny Compton	14 48	58.7
13.9	Milepost 92	17 52	54.9
19.8	BANBURY	22 45	72.4
24.9	Aynho Junc	27 15	68.0
29.2	Milepost 14	31 36	59.3
33.9	Bicester	35 52	66.2
43.2	Ashendon Junc	44 05	67.9
48.1	Milepost 29	48 30	66.7
55.1	Milepost 22	55 38	58.8
60.8	HIGH WYCOMBE	60 52	65.0
65.6	Beaconsfield	66 15	53.5
77.0	Northolt Junc	76 22	67.2
82.7	Park Royal	81 12	70.7
84.0	Old Oak West Junc	82 23	65.9
87.3	PADDINGTON	88 05	—

for the old route, which were slipped at Banbury, but the 12.13pm detached a portion at Leamington. The schedule of this train was then twenty-six minutes to Leamington and ninety-one minutes to Paddington. With the heavy load of nearly 300 tons time was kept to Leamington, and then speed was a little less than that of *Grosvenor* over the new line. This run was unfortunately made before Mr Goodyear began recording maximum and minimum speeds, though it is evident from the averages which I have worked out that the speed of *Melbourne* below Bicester did not approach the 77½mph of *Grosvenor* at this same point. The really superb part of *Melbourne*'s run was from Ashendon Junction to High Wycombe. Milepost 29 marks the end of the nearly level stretch, and allowing for the slack then required over Ashendon Junction the speed must have been well over 70mph on entering upon the climb over the Chilterns. Then such an average as 58.8mph over the seven adverse miles must have involved a minimum of little less than 55mph on the final stretch of 1 in 167. Passing High Wycombe in such good time, there was no need for any hurricane running down the Gerrards Cross bank, and with an undelayed finish Paddington was reached three minutes early. This is one of the finest runs I have ever seen with a City in ordinary service, and it fitly concludes the first volume of this historical account.

APPENDIX

ATBARA CLASS 4—4—0 : MAJOR DIMENSIONS

CYLINDERS:

diameter	18in
stroke	26in
thickness of metal	1in
centre to centre	27in
ports length, steam and exhaust	16in
ports width, steam	1 3/4in
ports width, exhaust	3in
port bridges width	1in

SLIDE VALVES:

length	17 3/4in
outside lap	1 1/8in
lead in full gear, forward	3/16in
lead in full gear, backward	1/4in
maximum travel	4 5/8in

CONNECTING RODS:

wrought iron, length	6ft 9in

ECCENTRIC RODS:

length between centres	5ft 9in
length to centre of pin	4ft 10 3/4in
sheaves, cast iron, throw	3 3/8in

FRAMES:

steel, length	29ft 6in
thickness	3/4in
distance between	4ft 1in

CRANK AXLE:

steel, hooped, diameter at middle	7 1/2in
crank pins	8in dia x 5in
journals inside	7 1/2in dia x 7in
journals inside between centres	4ft 0in
journals outside	7in dia x 8in
journals outside between centres	6ft 5in
wheel seat diameter	9in

TRAILING AXLE:

steel, diameter at middle	7in
journals	7 1/2in dia x 8in
journals between centres	6ft 5in
wheel seat diameter	9in

BOILER:

Barrel, steel, outside diameter	4ft 6 1/4in x 11ft 0in
Plates, thickness, barrel	9/16in
Plates, thickness, front tube plate	5/8in
Plates, thickness, firebox shell	9/16in
Firebox, copper, plates thickness:	
tube plates	3/4in and 9/16in
back, sides and roof	9/16in
Copper stays, at mean pitch of 3 3/4in	1in dia
Tubes:	
277, outside diameter	1 7/8in, thickness 10 swg and 12 swg
length between tube plates	11ft 3 13/16in
pitch	2 1/8in
Working pressure	180lb/sq in
Heating surfaces:	
Tubes	1540.18sq ft
Firebox	124.1sq ft
Total	1664.28 sq ft
Grate Area	21.28sq ft

LOCOMOTIVE WEIGHTS: in working order

On the bogie	18t 0c
On the driving axle	17t 8c
On the trailing axle	16t 4c

TENDER:

Weight loaded	33t 0c
Water capacity	3000 gallons
Coal space, without heaping	4 tons

The intervening stages between the dome boilered 7, 8, 14 and 16, and the hybrid Flowers of which the corresponding numbers were 4171, 4172, 4170 and 4169 show the way the policy of standardisation and interchangeability of boiler took its course; the case histories of the four locomotives, before they arrived at their final form are of more than usual interest:

No 7 *Armstrong*

March 1894	built Swindon Works
October 1905	Belpaire firebox, barrel 3/4-coned, drumhead smoke box
December 1911	superheated
February 1923	renumbered 4171
September 1928	withdrawn

No 8 *Gooch*

May 1894	built Swindon Works
November 1911	Belpaire firebox, barrel half-coned, drumhead smokebox superheated
April 1914	ditto but 3/4-coned boiler superheated
March 1917	ditto but 1/2-coned boiler superheated
January 1923	ditto but 3/4-coned boiler superheated
February 1923	renumbered 4172
April 1929	withdrawn

No 14 *Charles Saunders*

May 1894	built Swindon Works
September 1909	Belpaire firebox, barrel 3/4-coned, drumhead smoke-box
February 1911	superheated
May 1917	renumbered 4170
August 1928	withdrawn

No 16 *Brunel*

June 1894	built Swindon Works
September 1901	raised Belpaire firebox, straight barrel, domeless, curved smokebox
July 1909	Belpaire firebox, 3/4-coned barrel, drumhead smoke-box
June 1913	superheated
April 1915	renumbered 4169
July 1930	withdrawn

INDEX